QUICK REFERENCE GUIDE TO
31 SMALL STEPS TO ORGANIZE FOR EMERGENCIES (AND DISASTERS)

Shawndra Holmberg, CPO-CD®

books by
Shawndra Holmberg

31 Small Steps to Organize Your Life
31 Small Steps to Organize for Weight Loss
31 Small Steps to Organize Your Paper
31 Small Steps to Organize for Emergencies (and Disasters)

Table of Contents

what did you say this book was about?

For those of you who want to cut to the chase and skip the background information, this *Quick Reference Guide to 31 Small Steps to Organize for Emergencies (and Disasters)* is for you. It's the actions you need to take to be prepared for the next emergency, disaster, or zombie attack. I've kept the checklists and resources and left out the explanations, the reasons why, and the clarifications. This guide is the bare bones information you need.

disaster, emergency, or just the unexpected

When you think of emergencies and disasters, you may picture hurricanes, tornadoes, floods, or blizzards. This *Quick Reference Guide* is intended to help you be better prepared for those emergencies and disasters.

But a disaster does not have to affect your whole community. A disaster is **anything that overwhelms your resources**. Sometimes things can happen just to you or your family. It can be as routine as your car needing repair, a water heater that floods your basement, or gremlins in the attic. These steps will also prepare you for those more immediate and personal emergencies.

which emergencies and disasters?

Identify your top three hazards.

HAZARDS

- ❑ Active Shooter
- ❑ Bioterrorism
- ❑ Chemical Emergencies
- ❑ Cyber Security
- ❑ Dam/Levee Failures
- ❑ Drought
- ❑ Earthquakes
- ❑ Explosions
- ❑ Extreme Heat (heat wave)
- ❑ Floods
- ❑ Gremlins
- ❑ Hazardous Materials Incidents
- ❑ House Fires
- ❑ Household Chemical Emergencies
- ❑ Hurricanes
- ❑ Landslides and Debris Flow
- ❑ Nuclear Blast
- ❑ Nuclear Power Plants
- ❑ Pandemic
- ❑ Power Outages
- ❑ Radiation and Radiological Dispersion Device

- ❑ Severe Weather
- ❑ Snowstorms and Extreme Cold
- ❑ Space Weather (solar flares)
- ❑ Terrorism
- ❑ Thunderstorms and Lightning
- ❑ Tornadoes
- ❑ Tribbles
- ❑ Tsunamis
- ❑ Volcanoes and Lava Flow (volcanic eruption)
- ❑ Wildfires
- ❑ Zombies

Save Your Ones ($)

Pick ONE action to take today:

- ❑ Start saving your one-dollar bills until you collect $200

- ❑ Continue to save one-dollar bills until you reach your chosen limit

Possible Next Actions:

- ❑ Build up a savings fund for emergencies such as car repairs or a job loss. Your goal may be 3-6 months of expenses, but you can start small.

  This fund should be in an account separate from your normal everyday accounts so you don't dip into the reserve. Set your guidelines for use. You could decide that it's for the emergency repair on the car, home maintenance and preparedness, or a bigger emergency.

- ❑ Save 1% of your paycheck, then 5%, and build up to 10%. As most financial planners will tell you — pay yourself first when it comes to savings.

Fill Up Your Gas Tank at Half-empty

Pick ONE action to take today:

- ❏ Build the habit of filling your gas tank at half-full

Possible Next Actions:

- ❏ Check your tire pressure when you fill up

- ❏ Remind friends and family to fill their gas tanks at half-full

Lines of Communication

Pick ONE action to take today:

- ❑ Get a car charger for your cell phone — keep it in the car.

- ❑ Buy a Trimline corded phone if you have a landline — place it near your emergency lighting (Step #4) or near the phone outlet.

- ❑ Get a portable charger that can be recharged via a regular outlet or car charger. Add it to your Grab & Go checklist in Step #10.

Possible Next Actions:

- ❑ Buy a data blocking USB adaptor aka USB condom — add one to your emergency kit, travel kit, purse, briefcase, and more.

- ❑ Get an Uninterruptible Power Supply (UPS) for your VoIP system.

REDUCE POWER USAGE ON YOUR SMARTPHONE:

- Close all apps
- Turn off Wi-Fi
- Turn of apps accessing GPS location
- Lower brightness of screen
- Don't run down your car battery while using or charging your phone. Turn the engine on.

4

Light

Pick ONE action to take today:

- ❏ Add a flashlight or lantern to your emergency kit

Possible Next Actions:

- ❏ Get a flashlight or lantern for home, car, or travel

- ❏ Try out your lantern or flashlight

First Aid Kit

Pick ONE action to take today:

- ❑ Buy or build a first aid kit for your car
- ❑ Buy or build a first aid kit for the other cars

Possible Next Actions:

- ❑ Buy or build a first aid kit for your home
- ❑ Buy or build a first aid kit for your emergency kit
- ❑ Purchase a first aid book in print.
- ❑ Take a First Aid or CPR/AED training class. Providing first aid is not intended to replace medical treatment if the situation warrants it, but rather to provide immediate help. Check out your local Red Cross at www.redcross.org/about-us/our-work/training-education.

Resources:

- ❑ Poison Control Center: www.PoisonHelp.org 1-800-222-1222

ITEMS TO INCLUDE IN YOUR CAR'S KIT:

- ❑ Adhesive bandages, large strips
- ❑ Bandages, thumb or finger
- ❑ Bandages, 2-3 large square
- ❑ Bandage or adhesive tape
- ❑ Elastic bandage wrap, self-cling bandage wrap
- ❑ Antibiotic salve or spray
- ❑ Hydrocortisone or anti-itch cream
- ❑ Sunburn relief spray, gel or lotion
- ❑ Pain reliever

- ❑ Tweezers (blunt tipped, needle-nose pliers, or hemostats — to remove splinters and foreign object)

- ❑ Scissors

- ❑ Medicine dropper or needleless syringe

- ❑ Safety pins, a mix of medium and large

- ❑ Sterile saline wash (for cleaning wounds)

- ❑ Eye wash solution

- ❑ Hand sanitizer

- ❑ Moistened towelettes

- ❑ Non-latex disposable gloves

- ❑ Cold packs

- ❑ Heat packs

- ❑ Poison Control Center number: 1-800-222-1222 and online at www.PoisonHelp.org.

For the home kit, include all the previously listed items and add these:

- ❑ Anti-diarrhea medication

- ❑ Laxatives

- ❑ Syrup of ipecac to cause vomiting IF ADVISED by the Poison Control Center

- ❑ Activated charcoal to stop vomiting IF ADVISED by the Poison Control Center

- ❑ Bubble wrap for splinting

Some non-standard options I always have in my home first aid kit and routinely add when camping or traveling are:

- ❑ Arnica Montana salve and pills for bruises and muscle soreness.

- ❑ Ichthammol — drawing salve — for splinters, bug bites, etc. — STINKS and is messy but amazing!

Build an Emergency Kit — Get a Bag

Pick ONE action to take today:

- ❏ Find, get or buy one container for you or for your family to hold your emergency supplies.

Possible Next Actions:

- ❏ Build an individual kit for each family member.

- ❏ Build a kit to keep in your car; keep in mind temperature extremes that can affect some of the items you'll be adding to your emergency kit.

- ❏ Build a kit for every car in the family.

- ❏ Build a kit to keep at work.

Remember, the idea is to become better prepared, not do it all at one time (unless you have the time and money to do it all at once).

Details on each item in the Emergency Kit is in Appendix A.

Emergency Kit

- ❑ **Water*** (bottled or a water filter)
- ❑ **Medicine***
- ❑ **Cash**
- ❑ **Food** * **& Can Opener**
- ❑ **First Aid Kit & Guide**
- ❑ **Radio**
- ❑ **Flashlight**
- ❑ **Batteries**
- ❑ **Whistle**
- ❑ **Multi-purpose knife/tool**
- ❑ **Mask & Gloves** (at least 60% alcohol)
- ❑ **Hand Sanitizer**
- ❑ **Toilet Paper & Facial Tissues**
- ❑ **Personal Toiletries & Needs**
- ❑ **Change of Clothing**
- ❑ **PIC** (Personal Information Center notebook)
- ❑ **Extra Glasses**
- ❑ **Pencils, Pens, Games, Books, Paper, Toys**

* **enough for 3 days**
(or more)

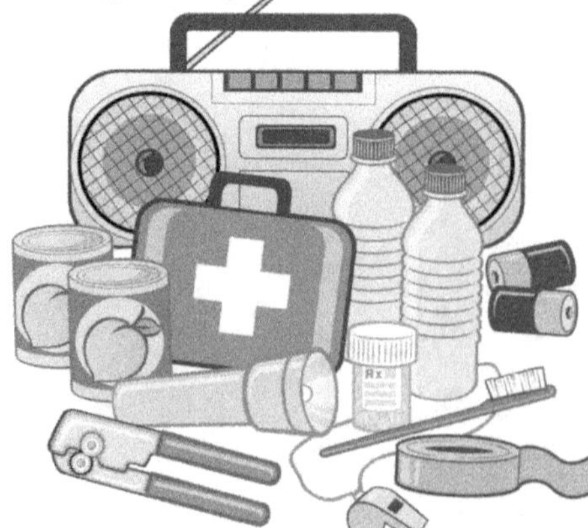

Records to put in your PIC

- ❑ **Inventory list for insurance**
- ❑ **Recent photo of each person**
- ❑ **Medical contact information**
- ❑ **Copies of bills & accounts**
- ❑ **Copies of important papers**
- ❑ **And more – see Step #11**

Build an Emergency Kit — Add Medications

Pick ONE action to take today:

- ❏ Check with your insurance company about getting more than a 30-day supply of your daily medicine

- ❏ Build the habit of ordering your prescription medicine before you get down to the last couple of pills

- ❏ Build an emergency Rx and OTC supply

Possible Next Actions:

- ❏ Add a list of medicine (Rx and OTC) to your Grab & Go list (Step #10)

- ❏ Ask your pharmacist about unused drug disposal programs or find a drug take back location in your community

Resources

- Expiration dates: www.health.harvard.edu/staying-healthy/drug-expiration-dates-do-they-mean-anything

- Local drug take back locations: takebackday.dea.gov

- Disposal: www.epa.gov/sites/production/files/2015-06/documents/how-to-dispose-medicines.pdf

- Disposal: www.fda.gov/ForConsumers/ConsumerUpdates/ucm101653.htm

KEEP OR TOSS EXPIRED MEDICATION

Expiration dates may not necessarily mean you need to toss it. Here are a few rules of thumb:

- If your life depends on it — toss expired medication.

- If it has changed color, consistency or odor — toss it regardless of expiration.

- Don't take the aspirin if it smells like vinegar. It's one medication that should always be tossed when expired, or sooner if it smells like vinegar.

- Store medication in a cool, dry environment. Your bathroom medicine cabinet is rarely a good place.

Build an Emergency Kit — Clothes and Hygiene

Pick ONE action to take today:

- ❑ Pack jeans and a t-shirt.

- ❑ Pack pajamas or clothes to sleep in.

- ❑ Add underwear and socks to your emergency kit.

- ❑ Build a travel kit with personal hygiene items and add it to your emergency kit.

- ❑ Add Rx glasses or cheaters.

Possible Next Actions:

- ❑ If you don't already have a pair of walking shoes (and socks) in the car for those opportunities of getting extra steps in when you're out and about, add them now. In the winter, you'll want to have a pair of boots in the car as well.

- ❑ If you live in a place that gets cold or snows, add in warmer items. Consider a cold-weather car kit that includes a jacket, boots, a hat, scarf, gloves, and a blanket. You'll be prepared to shelter in your car if you're stuck on the road.

- ❑ Refer to Appendix A for a more detailed list of items to include in your emergency kit.

INCLUDE PERSONAL HYGIENE ITEMS IN TRAVEL SIZE

- Shampoo, conditioner, soap, and lotion.

- Add a toothbrush, toothpaste. Does your dentist hand you a packet after a cleaning? Drop it in your kit.

- Feminine hygiene products if needed.

- Disposable shaver and cream.

- Include a wash cloth if you want and a "quick dry" towel. You may not normally use these but they'll be yours in an emergency shelter.

Prepare your Pets —
Build an Emergency Supply Kit

Pick ONE action to take today:

- ❑ Get a container to hold your pet's emergency supplies.

- ❑ Start building your pet emergency kit. Add to it over time.

- ❑ Make pulling from and restocking your pet's emergency kit a habit — "shop" your emergency kit. This rotates the supplies and keeps food and medication fresh.

- ❑ Buy a pet first aid book. Choose a print version first.

- ❑ Add the animal poison control number to your phone list.

Possible Next Actions:

- ❑ Add one more item to your pet's emergency kit.

- ❑ Check the contact information on your pet's tag. Update if necessary.

- ❑ Keep a leash in your vehicle. If you frequently travel with your dog in the car, keep a leash in the vehicle in case you have to vacate the car.

- ❑ Make a copy of your pet's records (vaccinations, microchip number, medicine, dietary needs) and keep a copy with the pet emergency supply kit.

Resources:

- • Dimensions for container: www.iata.org/whatwedo/cargo/live-animals/pets/Pages/index.aspx

- • Emergency muzzle: youtu.be/h8CwNyfaU3g

- • Birds, reptiles, horses, and small animals: www.aspca.org/pet-care/general-pet-care/disaster-preparedness

Emergency Supply Kit for Pets

❑ **Water*** (bottled)

❑ **Food*** (canned or stored in an airtight, waterproof container)

❑ **Can opener** (if stocking canned food)

❑ **Medication**** (stored in an airtight, waterproof container)

❑ **First aid kit** (or add pet items to your main kit)

❑ **First aid book for pets**   (my choice) ———→

❑ **Travel bag, carrier, or crate** (one for each pet)

❑ **Anti-anxiety vest or wrap** (for each pet)

❑ **Collar/harness and leash with tags** (cats/dogs)

❑ **Long leash and yard stake** (dogs)

❑ **Litter tray and litter** (cats)

❑ **Poop bags** (dogs)

❑ **Food & water bowls**

❑ **Toys**

* enough for 3 – 7 days
** enough for 2 weeks

Records to add

❑ **Vet records**

❑ **Recent photo of pet**

❑ **Microchip records**

❑ **Vet contact information**

PET FIRST AID KIT

Create a special pet first aid kit or add pet items to your main kit. In general, you'll want to have supplies to respond to:

Routine care needs:

- ❑ Nail clippers
- ❑ Styptic powder
- ❑ Scissors, round tipped
- ❑ Tweezers or needle-nose pliers
- ❑ Tick removal tool

Cuts, abrasions, foreign objects:

- ❑ Sterile saline solution
- ❑ Non-latex disposable gloves
- ❑ Cotton balls or swabs
- ❑ Antiseptic wipes, lotions, or spray
- ❑ Antibiotic ointment
- ❑ Gauze and non-stick bandages (self-sticking wrap)

Broken or sprained limbs

- ❑ Splints, tongue depressors, bubble wrap
- ❑ Self-sticking wrap, adhesive tape, even duct tape (to hold the splint in place — but don't get any hair stuck)
- ❑ Ice packs

Poisoning, allergic reactions — CALL VET or POISON CONTROL to confirm use, but have on hand

- ❑ Diphenhydramine (Benadryl®) for allergic reactions
- ❑ Hydrogen peroxide, 3%, if the vet or poison-control expert directs you to induce vomiting

❑ Syrup of Ipecac, if the vet or poison-control expert directs you to induce vomiting

❑ Poison Control Number

In addition to your vet's contact information, you'll want to have the Poison Control Number for animals. Have a credit card ready as a fee will usually apply.

- ASPCA Animal Poison Control Center Phone Number: **(888) 426-4435** (there's a fee)

- Pet Poison Helpline: **855-764-7661** (there's a fee)

Create Your Grab & Go Checklist

Pick ONE action to take today:

❑ Build your Grab & Go List

Possible Next Actions:

❑ Try the list out. Use it for packing for vacations, camping trips, picnics.

❑ Purchase refrigerator-freezer thermometer to monitor temperature.

YOUR GRAB & GO CHECKLIST

GRAB	**PREP**
Priority Items	**Priority Items**

GRAB

Priority Items

❑ Emergency Cash
❑ PIC Notebook
❑ Bill paying kit
❑ Passports & IDs
❑ Safety deposit key or home safe

Electronics

❑ Phones
❑ Phone chargers
❑ Batteries
❑ Flashlights & Lanterns
❑ Laptops & power cords
❑ iPads/Tablets & chargers
❑ Portable charger pack
❑ Camera & charger

Medication

❑ Prescription medication
❑ Any written prescriptions
❑ Medical equipment
❑ Pet medication
❑ Cold, Flu & Allergy medication
❑ Ibuprofen/Aspirin/Acetaminophen
❑ Supplements

PREP

Priority Items

❑ Gas up
❑ ATM — more cash
❑ Buy extra batteries

Electronics (if time)

❑ Charge phones
❑ Charge laptops
❑ Charge tablets
❑ Charge portable charger pack
❑ Forward home phone to cell phone, if applicable

Medication

❑ Charge batteries for medical equipment

GRAB	**PREP**

Clothing

 Clothing (PREP)

- ❑ Luggage
- ❑ Jeans, 1-2
- ❑ T-shirts, 1-2
- ❑ Long-sleeved shirt
- ❑ Pajamas
- ❑ Jacket or sweater
- ❑ Underwear
- ❑ Socks
- ❑ Walking shoes
- ❑ Flip flops
- ❑ Warm boots*
- ❑ Warm jacket*
- ❑ Hat and gloves*

* if winter

Comfort and Hygiene

- ❑ Pillows**
- ❑ Blankets** (or sleeping bag)
- ❑ Toothbrush and toothpaste
- ❑ Personal hygiene products
- ❑ Toilet paper
- ❑ Trash bags

** evacuation shelters may not have these

Dry Goods

- ❑ Coffee/Tea/Cocoa
- ❑ Sugar
- ❑ Canned meats
- ❑ Canned fruits
- ❑ Canned vegetables
- ❑ **Can opener**
- ❑ Peanut butter
- ❑ Crackers
- ❑ Individual snacks
- ❑ Water

Dry Goods (PREP)

- ❑ Fill water bottles

GRAB

**Refrigerated and
Frozen Foods**

- ❑ Cooler(s)
- ❑ Reusable ice packs
- ❑ Frozen foods easily cooked
- ❑ Fruits and vegetables
- ❑ Deli meats
- ❑ Cheeses
- ❑ Refrigerated foods that are safe if unrefrigerated for 4 hours or more

PREP

**Refrigerated and
Frozen Foods**

- ❑ Freeze all reusable ice packs
- ❑ Freeze additional bags or bottles of water, leave space for expansion
- ❑ Buy ice
- ❑ Put a thermometer in cooler to ensure safe temperatures are maintained***

*** refer to Appendix J (Refrigerated Foods) and Appendix K (Frozen Foods) for safe temperatures

Your Personal Information Center (PIC)

Pick ONE action to take today:

- ❑ Get a notebook and set of tabs. Start building your PIC.

- ❑ Choose an electronic platform and start build your electronic PIC (ePIC)

    Keep your hard copy PIC notebook and your ePIC secure

Possible Next Actions:

- ❑ Get a safe deposit box

- ❑ Get a fire and water-resistant home safe

- ❑ Update your Will. If you don't have one, get one.

- ❑ Update your Health Care Advance Directive (Living Will). If you don't have one, get one.

Resources:

- Password manager: 1password.com

- Password manager: www.lastpass.com

- How to stay safe online: staysafeonline.org/stay-safe-online/securing-key-accounts-devices/passwords-securing-accounts

BUILDING YOUR PIC

TAB #1 — PLANS

- ❑ Your Grab & Go checklist from Step #10;

- ❑ Your family communication plan from Steps #14 and #15;

- ❑ The emergency kit supply list from Step #6 (also in Appendix A); and

- ❑ The emergency supply list for your pets from Step #9 (also in Appendix B).

TAB #2 — PHOTOS

TABS #3 through#13 — DOCUMENTS

Add 11 tabs for the categories below and any additional tabs you choose.

- ❑ Bank Accounts
- ❑ Bills
- ❑ Credit Cards
- ❑ Digital Accounts
- ❑ Insurance
- ❑ Investments
- ❑ Medical
- ❑ Pets
- ❑ Property
- ❑ Safe Deposit Box
- ❑ Wills and Directives
- ❑ additional tabs you choose

Bank Accounts

- ❏ Checking / Share Draft / NOW
- ❏ Savings / Share
- ❏ Cash, amounts and locations (savings deposit box, emergency kit, coffee can in the back yard)
- ❏ CDs
- ❏ Money market accounts
- ❏ Revolving lines of credit attached to your checking
- ❏ Savings bonds

Bills

- ❏ Auto Registration
- ❏ Home Maintenance — Pest Protection / Security / Lawn Care
- ❏ Insurance bills/payments (copies of the policies will go under the Insurance tab)
  - ❏ Auto
  - ❏ Dental
  - ❏ Homeowners
  - ❏ Life
  - ❏ Renters
  - ❏ Medical
- ❏ Loans
- ❏ Magazine Subscriptions (not as important, but why not). Cut off the cover with the mailing label and three-hole punch it. Add it to this section
- ❏ Mortgage / Rent
- ❏ Property taxes
- ❏ Utilities
  - ❏ Cable/Internet
  - ❏ Electricity
  - ❏ Gas
  - ❏ Phone (Cell, Landline)
  - ❏ Sewer
  - ❏ Trash
  - ❏ Water

Credit Cards

- ❏ American Express
- ❏ Discover
- ❏ Visa / MasterCard
- ❏ Department Stores (Sears, Macy's, etc.)
- ❏ Gas

Digital Accounts — details in Step #12

Insurance – include policy statements (the bill statements go under the Bills tab)

- ❏ Auto
- ❏ Home / Renters
- ❏ Medical
- ❏ Dental
- ❏ Eye
- ❏ Accident
- ❏ Disability
- ❏ Life
- ❏ Pet medical

Investments

- ❏ 401(k)s
- ❏ Bonds
- ❏ Brokerage Accounts
- ❏ Businesses
- ❏ DRIPs
- ❏ IRAs
- ❏ Partnerships
- ❏ Retirement

Medical – you need a list of doctors, prescriptions, medical equipment, and provider contact information for every family member, but instead of writing all that down, add the Explanation of Benefits (EOB) report that your insurance provides or the doctor and facility bill statement.

- ❏ Primary care
- ❏ Specialists
- ❏ Dental
- ❏ Eye
- ❏ Home care
- ❏ Meals assistance
- ❏ Pharmacy — receipts and prescription information
- ❏ Medical equipment — receipts, maintenance or service agreements, operating instructions, repair and replacement information
- ❏ Allergies or health issues
- ❏ Recurring appointments (dialysis, oncology treatment, therapy, etc.)
- ❏ Vaccination records
- ❏ Date of last Tetanus shot ____________________

Pets

- ❏ Latest vet bill with vaccinations
- ❏ Health needs — receipts, vet bills, etc.
  - ❏ Allergies
  - ❏ Dietary needs
  - ❏ Medication
  - ❏ Treatments
- ❏ Microchip certificate
- ❏ Receipt from Pet Recovery Service
- ❏ Receipt from your pet sitter or day-care
- ❏ Photos of your pets (if you want additional ones here)

Property

- ❏ Property inventory list (aka home inventory, Step #26)
- ❏ Receipts for art or other big-ticket items
- ❏ Vehicle registrations (a copy of course or an old one)
- ❏ Other documentation

Safe Deposit Box – add a copy to your PIC

- ❐ Birth certificates
- ❐ Death certificates
- ❐ Deeds
- ❐ Digital accounts list (Step #12)
- ❐ Divorce certificates
- ❐ Irreplaceable memorabilia
- ❐ Life insurance policies
- ❐ Passports
- ❐ Property inventory (include photos, video, certificate of ownership, etc.)
- ❐ Retirement Account Information
- ❐ Social Security cards
- ❐ Wedding certificates

Add a list of other items you have in your safe deposit box

- ❐ ___________________________
- ❐ ___________________________
- ❐ ___________________________

Add:

- ❑ Location of safe deposit box
- ❑ Location of safe deposit box key
- ❑ Box #:
- ❑ Signatories
- ❑ Security requirements

If you don't have a safe deposit box consider a fire safe.

Wills and Directives

- ❐ Last Will and Testament
- ❐ Health Care Advance Directive
- ❐ Power-of-Attorney
- ❐ Trusts
- ❐ Location of originals: ___________________________

The original copies should be kept in a safe place. A safe deposit box is not a good place for wills or directives as your executor may not be able to access it unless they are signatories on the box.

Your Digital Accounts — List Them

Pick ONE action to take today:

- ❑ Decide whether you're going digital or paper with your list of digital accounts and how you'll keep the information secure.

- ❑ Start your list of accounts. Keep it secure. ☺

- ❑ Add to your list of accounts. Keep it secure. ☺ ☺

Possible Next Actions:

- ❑ Go to Appendix D — Digital Estate Planning to learn about assigning legacy contacts, inactive account managers, and other options for developing a Digital Estate Plan.

Include the following information for each account on your list:

- Name of Account

- Website URL

- Payment information. Include how often you're charged, how you pay (credit card, bank account, invoiced, or automatic debit, etc.)

- If you access the account from an app on your phone, tablet or computer, note which device and app name.

- Use or reason for the account, i.e. personal email, social media page for business, emergency fund, receive payment from..., etc.

- Additional individuals on the account or with account access.

Examples of service and product accounts to include are:

- ❑ Data storage (Dropbox, Box, Google Drive, iCloud, OneDrive, backup applications, computers, external hard drives, etc.)

- ❑ Devices (computers, laptops, phone, tablet, etc.). Though these may not be "accounts", you might use a password to lock the device. And they definitely contain data. Include these.

- ❑ Email (Gmail, Yahoo, Outlook etc.)

- ❑ Entertainment (Netflix, Acorn, Vudu, Hulu, Amazon, CBS, NBC, ABC, etc.)

- ❑ Home inventory (spreadsheet on your computer, an app on your phone, or an account on the web, etc.). The paper version of your home inventory list would be located behind the **Property** tab in your PIC.

- ❑ Photo storage and organizing accounts (Google, iCloud, Costco, Forever, Dropbox, etc.)

- ❑ Shopping accounts (Amazon, eBay, Etsy, etc.)

- ❑ Social Media (Facebook, Twitter, Snapchat, Goodreads, Instagram, Pinterest, Google+, etc.) Note if your credit card or bank account is attached.

- ❑ Utilities (internet, phone, cell phone, etc.) if you didn't already include them in your PIC under the **Bills** tab

- ❑ Websites, blogs, and domains you own

Include financial accounts if you didn't already include them in your PIC under the **Bank Accounts** and **Investments** tabs. Accounts such as:

- ❑ Bank Accounts

- ❑ Investment accounts

- ❑ Retirement Accounts

You may also have additional assets to list:

- ❑ Books you've published (CreateSpace, KDP, iTunes, Barnes & Noble Nook, Kobo, Smashwords, Amazon Author Page, Ingram, publishers, agent, etc.).

- ❑ eCommerce sites for your products, services, creations, and more (eBay, Etsy, auction sites, online art galleries, classified ad sites such as Craigslist, etc.).

- ❑ Income producing accounts that provide passive income (affiliates programs, YouTube, online training sites, etc.).

- ❑ Merchant accounts (PayPal, QuickBooks, Square, etc.).

- ❑ Social Media (Facebook, Snapchat, Instagram, etc.). Yes, social media accounts may have income associated with them. Did you set up a Buy button on your business page or use the peer-to-peer (P2P) payment system to get the cost of that ticket from your friend? Note it.

  Also record if the accounts automatically transfer the money to your bank account or if it has to be done manually. Include which accounts are connected.

13 — Take Updated Photos of Family and Pets

Pick ONE action to take today:

- ❑ Take pictures of your pets and family members.

- ❑ Print out a few pictures and add to your PIC (Step #11)

Make a Plan — Meetup

Pick ONE action to take today:

- ❑ Decide on a neighborhood meeting location.
- ❑ Determine a meetup location outside of town.

Possible Next Actions:

- ❑ Schedule a game night with the family and play *what-if*.
- ❑ Schedule a date to meet at your spot to get familiar with it. Make it fun!
- ❑ Ask your company or school when the next evacuation drill is and join in with a discussion at home about it.

Make a Plan — Check-In

Pick ONE action to take today:

- ❑ Identify your out-of-town contact. And tell your family.

- ❑ Add contact name and number(s) to your phones.

- ❑ Add the information to your emergency communication plan.

- ❑ Make a hard copy of the contact information and carry it in your backpack, purse, or wallet.

- ❑ Of course, let the contact know ☺

Possible Next Actions:

- ❑ Add 'ICE' contact(s) to phones.

- ❑ Determine your social media communication plan and share it with family.

- ❑ Create a written Family Communication Plan using the template. Add your meeting places from Step #14 (Make a Plan — Meetup).

- ❑ Create a neighborhood plan and call list to ensure that anyone who needs additional assistance due to age, mobility, or other challenges is taken care of during an emergency. We are stronger together than we are on our own.

Family Communication Plan

Texts are more likely to get through.
Call 911 if it's an emergency

HOUSEHOLD INFORMATION

Home Phone: _______________________

Name: _______________________________________
Cell: _______________ Email: _____________________
Social Media: _________________________________
Other Information: _____________________________
____

Name: _______________________________________
Cell: _______________ Email: _____________________
Social Media: _________________________________
Other Information: _____________________________
____

Name: _______________________________________
Cell: _______________ Email: _____________________
Social Media: _________________________________
Other Information: _____________________________
____

Name: _______________________________________
Cell: _______________ Email: _____________________
Social Media: _________________________________
Other Information: _____________________________
____

Pet: _________   Pet: _________   Pet: _________
Description: Description: Description:

Where Will You Meet?

In the Neighborhood: _______________________
Address: _____________________________________

In Town: _________________________________
Address: _____________________________________

Out of Town: ______________________________
Address: _____________________________________

Who's Your Contact?

Local: ___________________________________
Home: _______________ / Cell: ________________
Email: _______________ / Social Media: _________

Out-of-Town: _____________________________
Home: _______________ / Cell:_________________
Email: _______________ / Social Media: _________

WORK & SCHOOL

Work: _______________________________________
Address: _____________________________________
Phone: ______________________________________
Social Media: _________________________________
Emergency Plan/Pick-up: ________________________

Work: _______________________________________
Address: _____________________________________
Phone: ______________________________________
Social Media: _________________________________
Emergency Plan/Pick-up: ________________________

School: ______________________________________
Address: _____________________________________
Phone: ______________________________________
Social Media: _________________________________
Emergency Plan/Pick-up: ________________________

School: ______________________________________
Address: _____________________________________
Phone: ______________________________________
Social Media: _________________________________
Emergency Plan/Pick-up: ________________________

More Household Information

You can also use this for family
in another household

Name: _______________________________
Cell: _______________ Email: _______________
Social Media: _______________________________
Other Information: _______________________________
____

Name: _______________________________
Cell: _______________ Email: _______________
Social Media: _______________________________
Other Information: _______________________________
____

Name: _______________________________
Cell: _______________ Email: _______________
Social Media: _______________________________
Other Information: _______________________________
____

Name: _______________________________
Cell: _______________ Email: _______________
Social Media: _______________________________
Other Information: _______________________________
____

Pet: _______   Pet: _______   Pet: _______
Description: Description: Description:

Are You a Contact for Someone?

Name: _______________________________
Phone: _______________ / Social Media: _________
Email: _______________________________

Other Important Numbers

Child Care: _______________________________
Address: _______________________________
Phone: _______________________________
Social Media: _______________________________
Emergency Plan/Pick-up: _______________________

Senior Care: _______________________________
Address: _______________________________
Phone: _______________________________
Social Media: _______________________________
Emergency Plan/Pick-up: _______________________

Friend: _______________________________
Neighbor: _______________________________
Doctor: _______________________________
Doctor: _______________________________
Doctor: _______________________________
Pharmacy: _______________________________
Dentist: _______________________________
Vet: _______________________________
Kennel: _______________________________
Poison Control: 1.800.222.1222

_______________ : _______________________
_______________ : _______________________
_______________ : _______________________
_______________ : _______________________

Microchip Your Pets

Pick ONE action to take today:

- ❑ Microchip your pet

- ❑ Register your pet's microchip

- ❑ Confirm contact information is current

Possible Next Actions:

- ❑ Check the chip each year (August 15, annual vet visit, or check with your local humane society)

Resources:

- ❑ Universal Pet Microchip Lookup Tool at www.petmicrochiplookup.org.

Shelter in Place

Pick ONE action to take today:

- ❑ Choose a room for shelter based on your top three hazards.

- ❑ Choose ONE item to add to your emergency kit or shelter.

- ❑ Choose ONE action to prepare your home for your #1 hazard.

Possible Next Actions:

- ❑ Plan and prepare to shelter in place at work.

- ❑ Create a commuter emergency plan for the commute between home and work, school or shopping.

- ❑ Plan and prepare for kids to shelter in place at school. Find out what your schools' plans are and how they practice.

- ❑ Plan and prepare to shelter in your vehicle. Get an emergency kit for the car. NOTE: a vehicle should be a last resort for sheltering in place. It can be a dangerous place during some hazards such as high wind events and floods. Go to www.ready.gov/tornadoes to learn more about using a vehicle as shelter in a tornado.

- ❑ When traveling, make a habit of identifying where you might shelter in an emergency. Some airports have tornado shelters. Start a 'what-if' conversation with your hotel staff about local hazards and plans.

Resources:

- ❑ Building a safe room:
    - ○ www.fema.gov/safe-rooms
    - ○ www.fema.gov/residential-safe-rooms

- ❑ Commuter emergency plan:
  www.fema.gov/media-library-data/1390856235302-ff6e316df62851d5a5afe834b4fcd53c/Commuter_Emergency_Plan_v7_508.pdf

- ❑ Individuals with Disabilities: www.ready.gov/individuals-access-functional-needs

GATHER SUPPLIES TO SHELTER FROM ANY HAZARD

For all situations:

- ❑ The emergency kit you've been building (Step #6).

- ❑ A whistle

- ❑ Food & Water

- ❑ Duct tape

- ❑ NOAA Weather Radio

- ❑ First aid kit

- ❑ Blankets and pillows

- ❑ Sanitary supplies for pets:
  - o litter and box for cats,
  - o puppy pads or newspapers for dogs,
  - o plastic bags, bleach, paper towels

- ❑ Sanitary supplies for people if there's no bathroom available.
  - o 5-gallon bucket
  - o Heavy-duty plastic trash bags (use two at a time)
  - o Cat litter
  - o Snap-on toilet seat and lid made for 5-gallon buckets
  - o Toilet paper or moist towelettes
  - o Moist towelettes and hand-sanitizer
  - o Twist ties or zip ties

ACTIONS TO TAKE FOR ANY HAZARD

Well Before — when there's no emergency or disaster

- ❑ If you use medical equipment in your home that requires electricity, talk to your doctor or health care provider about how you can prepare for its use during a power outage.

- ❑ Talk with your insurance agent about your insurance needs.

- ❑ Continue to prepare your house and your family.

- ❑ Learn how to safely shut off your utilities. Step #29 (Get Trained / Get Involved).

- ❑ Have fire extinguishers available and ensure everyone is trained on how to use them.

Before — hours or days before the storm is due to hit your area

- ❑ Listen to your radio and check your FEMA or National Weather Service (NWS) phone apps for updates.

- ❑ Fill up your car (Step #2).

- ❑ Get money from your ATM/bank. Increase your cash on hand.

- ❑ Charge all phones and electronics.

- ❑ Charge all batteries for radios, flashlights, medical equipment, etc. And buy more batteries if needed.

- ❑ Turn your refrigerator and freezers to coldest setting. If power is lost during the storm, in order to maintain the temperature for as long as possible, do not open them unless necessary.

- ❑ Increase ice production and freeze all reusable ice packs.

- ❑ Freeze additional bags or bottles of water if you have room. Leave an inch or more of space in the bottle or bag for expansion of the ice.

- ❑ Fill food-grade containers with drinking water, if you don't already have your emergency water supply. See Step #21 (Water) for details.

- ❑ Fill all other containers with water for non-potable water needs. See Step #21 (Water) for details.

- ❑ Unplug all unnecessary appliances.

❑ Get emergency kit and emergency supplies, if not already present.

❑ Review your plans for meeting locations (Step #14), checking-in (Step #15), and evacuating (Steps #18 and #19).

❑ Bring in outside animals if possible.

During — you could be sheltering in place for a couple of hours or several days.

❑ Close and lock doors and windows. Though not routinely mentioned, locking may provide more stability to the window or door during high winds and a tighter seal against outside air.

❑ Continue to listen to your radio for updates and an all-clear announcement. Your FEMA or NWS phone app may provide updates, but it also drains your phone's battery. If there is a power outage, reserve your phone's battery for calls and texts. See Step #3 (Lines of Communication) for other ways to conserve your phone's power.

After — the storm has ended and recovery starts.

❑ Stay safe and aware of your surroundings.

❑ Shut off utilities if necessary and safe to do so.

❑ Begin the recovery process, see Step #30 (Prep for Recovery).

❑ Check on your neighbors.

PREPARATIONS TO MAKE FOR SPECIFIC HAZARDS

Earthquakes

You won't be "sheltering in place" during an earthquake as there is no warning. However, the Federal Emergency Management Agency (FEMA) offers a checklist for homeowners to hunt down and mitigate potential hazards. Consider the following:

- ❑ Purchase earthquake insurance — call your insurance company.

- ❑ Secure top-heavy furniture to wall studs with straps.

- ❑ Secure electronics, fish tanks, heavy objects that can fall, and items hanging on walls (mirrors, pictures, etc.) with flexible nylon straps, closed hooks, adhesives, or earthquake putty.

- ❑ Remove any items placed above beds or seating areas.

- ❑ Secure cabinet doors and drawers with child-proof latches to keep them closed and the contents inside.

- ❑ Secure water heaters, refrigerator, and other appliances with straps or braces — call a contractor.

- ❑ Brace chimneys — call a contractor.

- ❑ Use flexible gas line and appliance connections — call a qualified plumber.

- ❑ Strengthen weak crawlspace walls — call a contractor.

- ❑ For more information on strengthening new and existing homes, check out FEMA's Homebuilders' Guide to Earthquake-Resistant Design and Construction, www.fema.gov/media-library/assets/documents/6015

During

1. DROP to the ground

2. COVER your head and neck with your arms

   - If you can move safely, crawl for additional cover such as a sturdy table or an interior wall (away from windows).

3. HOLD ON until shaking stops

Floods

Though you're not likely to "shelter in place" during a flood either, here are some actions to take well before a flood threatens your home:

- ❏ Consider your risk. Are you located in a low-lying area near a river or stream, on the coast, downstream of a dam or levee, or in a flood zone?

- ❏ Look at the risk differently. If you're in a 100-year floodplain, your risk isn't just every 100 years. There's a one in five chance that a flood will occur in the next 25 years.[1]

- ❏ Purchase flood insurance — call your insurance company.

- ❏ Make a plan to get to higher ground. Establish more than one route for evacuation.

- ❏ Making structural changes to your home in order to reduce the flood risk will require professional help. Check out the FEMA document, *FEMA P-1037, Reducing Flood Risk to Residential Buildings That Cannot Be Elevated (2015),* www.fema.gov/media-library/assets/documents/109669

- ❏ Avoid walking or driving through flood waters. Six inches of moving water can knock you off your feet. A foot of water can sweep your vehicle away.

Hurricanes

Federal Emergency Management Agency (FEMA) offers a checklist for homeowners to avoid hurricane risks that include:

Well Before

- ❏ Purchase hurricane and/or flood insurance — call your insurance company.

- ❏ Install hurricane straps or clips to help keep your roof in place and connected to the walls in high winds — call a contractor.

- ❏ Install and maintain storm shutters or use 5/8-inch thick exterior-grade plywood sheets to cover windows and glass doors — call a contractor.

- ❏ Reinforce your garage door with heavier brackets to the glider wheel track and by adding hardware across the back of the door or replace it with a door that is approved for both wind pressure and impact protection — call your garage door expert.

---

[1] Robert Meyer, Howard Kunreuther, *The Ostrich Paradox: Why We Underprepare for Disasters,* Kindle Edition, Loc 632

- ❑ Remove trees that could fall on your home. If you're planting trees, keep in mind what its full-grown height will be and plant it at least that far away from your house.

- ❑ FEMA also has guidance documents for building a residential safe room to protect you from extreme windstorms (hurricanes and tornadoes) so you can shelter in place.

Before

- ❑ Anchor or remove potential windborne objects like trash cans, yard furniture, barbecue grills, playground equipment, and more. Anchor storage sheds.

- ❑ Close the storm shutters or put up the plywood sheets over windows and glass doors.

- ❑ Tape glass windows on the inside with large Xs to reduce shattering. This lessens the hazard of flying glass debris. Use shipping tape if possible. Duct tape will work but may be difficult to remove.

- ❑ Draw curtains and blinds. Again, this reduces the hazard of flying debris.

- ❑ Go Low! If you have the option of multiple shelters in your home, go low. However, if your home is in a flood zone and might be flooded during a hurricane, thunderstorm or other severe weather event, you don't want to be trapped by storm waters.

Tornadoes

You will need to shelter during a tornado. In addition to the structure reinforcements for hurricane preparedness above, consider the following actions for tornadoes:

Well Before

- ❑ If you don't have a safe room built to FEMA criteria to shelter in, the next best choice is a small, windowless, interior room on the lowest level.

- ❑ If you live or work in a mobile home, identify another nearby shelter or structure that can withstand the high winds.

During

- ❑ While sheltering, use a sturdy table and blankets, pillows or a heavy coat to provide additional protection.

- ❑ Cover your head and neck with your arms.

Winter Storms
(snowstorms and extreme cold)

Snowstorms and extreme cold can keep you homebound for days, and power outages are always a concern. Watch or listen for the weather reports in your area and take precautions before the storm hits.

❑ Ensure your home is well insulated BEFORE winter.

❑ Add weather stripping around doors and windows. Identify other areas that may need additional TEMPORARY insulation or coverage (with a blanket or plastic sheeting) such as pet doors, dryer vents, or even rooms.

❑ Know how to shut off the water in case of a burst pipe.

❑ Keep the pipes from freezing by turning the water on at a slow run or trickle (more than just a drip).

❑ Determine how you can stay warm if the power goes out. Your gas furnace probably requires electricity, so be prepared with:

　　o Additional blankets, sleeping bags, and warm winter coats.

　　o If you have a wood-burning stove or fireplace, stock plenty of firewood.

　　o If you have a gas fireplace, determine if yours uses a 'standing pilot' or an 'intermittent pilot'. The standing pilot is always lit and doesn't require electricity but the intermittent pilot does. Some of the energy saving gas fireplaces have a battery back-up. Verify your system before the storm hits.

❑ Do NOT use a gasoline generator, or a propane, natural gas, wood or charcoal burning grill, stove, or other device inside. They generate carbon monoxide and are fire hazards. A wood-burning stove or fireplace or a gas fireplace installed by a professional is exempt because proper ventilation has been installed and is set-up to code.

❑ Install carbon monoxide monitors in central locations on every level and outside of sleeping areas. If your monitors are hard wired, remember to change out the batteries at least annually to ensure the monitors continue to work during a power outage.

❑ Have fire extinguishers available and ensure everyone is trained on how to use them.

❑ Keep your exhaust vents free and clear of snow. This includes furnace, hot water heater, and other appliances.

Cold or flu
(a disaster is bad enough but what if you're sick too)

❑ Stock your pantry with at least a two-week supply of food.

❑ Have any nonprescription drugs and other health supplies on hand. Don't wait to get sick to buy them. Include:

- pain relievers,
- stomach remedies,
- cough and cold medicines,
- fluids with electrolytes, and
- vitamins.

❑ Have other items you use during an illness, including

- hand soap,
- facial tissues,
- hand-sanitizer, at least 60% alcohol,
- latex gloves, and
- disposable facemask.

❑ Practice good personal health habits NOW

- Stay home when you're sick.
- Stay home at least another 24 hours after you no longer have a fever (without the use of meds).
- Cover your coughs and sneezes with a tissue or your sleeve.
- Wash your hands, front and back and under your nails, with soap and water for at least 20 seconds. Hum the 'happy birthday song' twice.
- Clean frequently touched surfaces and objects. These can include faucet handles, door knobs, stair rails, remote controls, etc.

Community Shelter

Pick ONE action to take today:

- ❑ Create or update your Grab & Go checklist. This list can double as your vacation or camping packing list. Test it out and update when you get back each time.

- ❑ Add books, games, and puzzles to your emergency kit. Use physical products and not just apps on your phone.

Possible Next Actions:

- ❑ Try out your portable power supply to make sure you know how it works. Purchase one if you haven't already.

- ❑ Add a power strip to your emergency kit. This allows more than one person to charge their devices at a time and is very handy at a shelter.

WHEN YOU GO…

- ☐ Take your emergency kit, your PIC and all the supplies on your Grab & Go checklist. The following should already be on your checklist, but if not, add them to it.

- ☐ Bring your pillow and a blanket or sleeping bag.

- ☐ Pack clothes or pajamas to sleep in

- ☐ Change of clothes and clean underwear.

- ☐ If you have time and space to add in stadium chairs or folding chairs, do it.

- ☐ travel-size laundry soap to your emergency kit to do basic laundry in the sink.

Under the American with Disabilities Act, ADA, shelters are required to allow service animals remain with the individual served, but you will be required to take care and maintain control of the animal. You will need to provide food, water, medical and hygiene needs for your service animal.

Pets may or may not be allowed in or near the shelter, so be prepared. Preparing to take care of your animals and pets is next in Step #19 (Shelter for Your Animals) and Step #20 (Provide a Safe Cave for Your Pets — Get a Kennel for Each).

Shelter for Your Animals

Pick ONE action to take today:

- ❑ Identify where you, your family and your pets might shelter if you need to evacuate. Will it be with friends and family? Or will you need to find alternative shelter?

- ❑ Update your pet's vaccinations. Add shots for boarding.

Possible Next Actions:

- ❑ Continue to build your pet's emergency supplies (Step #9).

- ❑ Get your pet comfortable with traveling in the car. Take them on rides to dog parks, walks, doggie day care or anywhere that isn't the vet.

- ❑ Investigate sheltering options for you and your pet in a 100-mile radius. Print a list and include it in your PIC and pet's emergency supply kit. Consider:

  - Family and friends,

  - Hotels that allow household pet(s),

  - Boarding kennels,

  - Animal shelters and humane societies,

  - Veterinary offices with boarding facilities,

  - Grooming shops, and

  - Approved areas at fairgrounds or parks.

20

Provide a Safe Cave for Your Pets — Get a Kennel for Each

Pick ONE action to take today:

- ❑ Get a kennel for each pet.

- ❑ Work with your pet to make it a safe, relaxing place.

Possible Next Actions:

- ❑ If your pets don't use their kennels every day, bring them out every few months to reintroduce them.

- ❑ Discuss *what-if* scenarios for your pets.

Resources:

- Dimensions for container: www.iata.org/whatwedo/cargo/live-animals/pets/Pages/index.aspx

Water

Pick ONE action to take today:

- ❏ Decide how much water you will store.

- ❏ Clear space for your emergency water supply.

- ❏ Buy a case of bottled water per person (and pet) in household.

- ❏ Get food-grade water containers for collecting water.

- ❏ Freeze several bottles of water (leaving an inch or more of space for expansion).

Possible Next Actions:

- ❏ Buy unscented liquid household bleach (5-6% or 8.25% of sodium hypochlorite with nothing else added) for disinfecting the water and cleaning.

- ❏ Purchase a water filtration system, whether personal size or for the household, that doesn't require power.

- ❏ Try out your water filter. Don't just buy it and put it on a shelf. Put it together, run water through it. Test it out. Don't wait for an emergency to figure out how it works.

Resources:

- Water: www.ready.gov/water

- Water: www.cdc.gov/healthywater/emergency/drinking/creating-storing-emergency-water-supply.html

- See Appendix H — Safe Drinking Water for more details.

22

Choose Your Food

Pick ONE action to take today:

- ❑ Create a checklist of staples to always have on hand.

- ❑ Read the label and directions before purchasing packaged emergency foods.

- ❑ Add a manual can opener to your emergency kit. Buy one that is easy to use. Ensure everyone can operate it.

- ❑ Add a 3-day supply of portable, easy- or no-cook foods to your emergency kit.

Possible Next Actions:

- ❑ Go for seven days — once you have three days' worth of portable, easy- or no-cook foods, add four more days. Do you want more canned meat, fruit, and veggies, or shelf-stable milk, soup, crackers, granola, trail mix, etc.?

- ❑ Stock your pantry for 2- to 3-weeks' worth of meals. It doesn't have to be no-cook foods. It can be your usual items that you consume, but now there's no last-minute shopping needs.

- ❑ Alternative cooking methods — Look at other cooking appliances you have, such as your outdoor grill or your camp stove (use both outside). Try a solar oven. You can purchase them online or find instructions to make your own.

KEY FACTORS TO CONSIDER:

- Shelf life

- Salt content

- Nutrient content

- Serving size for each packet

- Water requirement

23

Build Your Emergency Stash from What You Have

Pick ONE action to take today:

- ❑ Pull out and check your camping gear. Store it together in an easy access location.
- ❑ Buy a cooler that you can manage by yourself.
- ❑ Fill your propane bottle or get another bag of charcoal for your grill.
- ❑ Freeze a jug or several bottles of water.
- ❑ Restock your car's first aid kit and food stash.
- ❑ Choose another action that will let your emergency stash do double duty.

Possible Next Actions:

- ❑ Build a car emergency kit, see Appendix N. Keep it stocked with healthier foods. It will be there for emergencies and is an option before you go shopping or if you're running late and need some energy.

Resources:

- • Coolers: www.outdoorgearlab.com/topics/camping-and-hiking/best-cooler/buying-advice

CAMPING GEAR FOR EMERGENCIES

❑ Backpacks	❑ Sleeping bags
❑ Cookware	❑ Sleeping pads
❑ Cooler and blue ice packs	❑ Stove
❑ Cups	❑ Utensils
❑ Lighting — Headlamps, lanterns, and flashlights.	❑ Water filter
❑ Shelter (tents or tarps),	❑ Water bottles
	❑ What else?

Extras — Pick ONE

Pick ONE action to take today:

- ❑ Pick one of the above items to do or add to your supplies.

Possible Next Actions:

- ❑ Pick another one.

ADDITIONAL ITEMS TO ADD TO YOUR KIT — PICK ONE

- ❑ Check out Appendix A — Emergency Kit Supply List and add ONE more item
- ❑ Check out Appendix B — Emergency Kit for Pets and add ONE more item.
- ❑ Duct tape
- ❑ Tarp(s)
- ❑ Work gloves
- ❑ Power strip
- ❑ Paper plates, cups and plastic utensils
- ❑ Plastic trash bags

ADDITIONAL PLANNING AND PREP — PICK ONE

- ❑ Memorabilia
- ❑ NOAA Weather Radio
- ❑ Buy a pre-paid mobile phone on a different carrier
- ❑ Carry a whistle
- ❑ Find and practice using the manual release lever on your garage door opener
- ❑ Identify the Exits
- ❑ Replace your smoke alarm batteries

❑ Take a senior safe driving course if you eligible

❑ Have a tire sealant in the car to fix flats. Read the instructions and follow the instructions BEFORE using.

❑ Check your auto insurance for roadside services

❑ Get printed maps of your area

❑ Hurricane clips

❑ Spray paint & permanent markers to mark your location, leave a message for responders that animals are present or have been evacuated, or other communication needs.

❑ Toilet paper

Update Your Tetanus Shot

Pick ONE action to take today:

- ❑ Get a tetanus shot or booster.

Possible Next Actions:

- ❑ If your tetanus booster is up-to-date, check what other vaccinations you might need. Find the recommended immunizations for adults at www.cdc.gov/vaccines/schedules/easy-to-read/adult.html.

- ❑ Get your annual flu shot unless your doctor suggests otherwise. The first week in December is usually National Influenza Vaccination Week, but get your flu shot earlier if you can.

Resources:

- Immunizations: ww.cdc.gov/vaccines/schedules/easy-to-read/adult.html

26 Home Inventory

Pick ONE action to take today:

- ☐ Take a quick walk around your house and video the rooms.

- ☐ Take a longer walk around the house, open drawers, cabinets, and closet doors and record it all on your smartphone. Talk about the items.

- ☐ Take pictures if you don't have video capabilities.

- ☐ Take pictures of your receipts, owner's manuals, evaluations, etc. to provide more details.

- ☐ Upload your inventory video and photos to a secure cloud storage.

- ☐ Make a copy (CD, DVD, flash drive or paper) of your inventory and store it in a secure off-site location.

Possible Next Actions:

- ☐ Add more information to your quick and easy inventory with video and photos showing more details.

- ☐ Review your insurance policy.

- ☐ Talk with your insurance agent to make sure you're paying for the right amount of insurance. There's no need to pay for more than you need, but you don't want to face the unwelcome realization that you didn't have the coverage you thought. It's estimated that 70% or more of the homes damaged in Texas and Louisiana from Hurricane Harvey didn't have flood insurance.[2]

- ☐ If you don't have insurance, consider it.

- ☐ Check out your insurance company's website to see if they have home inventory tools you can use, such as phone apps or checklists, such as:

---

[2] Leslie Scism and Nicole Friedman, Wall Street Journal, *Houston Residents Return Home to Scary Reality: No Insurance Coverage*, September 1, 2017, www.wsj.com/articles/houston-residents-return-home-to-scary-reality-no-insurance-coverage-1504300222

- o   Allstate's Digital Locker® app for iOS and Android

- o   Liberty Mutual Insurance has the Home Gallery® app for iOS

- o   Safeco Home Inventory app for iOS

- o   State Farm has checklists you can use

- ❑   If you want a more detailed home inventory you can:

  - o   keep it simple with electronic spreadsheet software (Microsoft Excel, Apache OpenOffice Calc, LibreOffice Calc, or Google Sheets);

  - o   write it down on paper and add it to your PIC from Step #11 (Take Your PIC — Personal Information Center); or

  - o   choose a software program by looking at the reviews online. One must-have capability of any program is the option to export the information into a spreadsheet in case the software is no longer supported or you want to move it to another platform.

NEXT — A DETAILED INVENTORY

Once you've made your basic video or taken pictures, you'll need to create a home inventory. You can either make a simple written list, use a spreadsheet or word-processing software, or utilize a home inventory app. You will want to include the following:

- Brand name

- Model number

- Description

- Where and when purchased

- Cost of purchase

- Replacement value

- Serial number on electronics

- Size for artwork, area rugs, computers and tv

- Warranties or maintenance contract

WHAT YOU'LL NEED TO FILE A CLAIM

- A list of items — yes, a home inventory will ultimately require a list, but a video is a great record to start with so that in the event you have to make a list, you don't have to do it from memory.

- Photos or video of your property and assets.

- Receipts for big ticket items.

- Appraisals for valuable items.

Backup — Computers and Files

Pick ONE action to take today:

- ❏ Get a safe deposit box or a fire safe for your vital and important documents.

- ❏ Choose one paper/hardcopy category to back up and take action on it today. Whether it's scanning/copying it yourself or hiring someone else to scan it — decide and take the first step to make it happen.

- ❏ Decide how you will back up your computer and take action.

- ❏ If you've decided on manual (versus automatic) backup — back up today! Schedule your next backup and commit to doing it.

Possible Next Actions:

Additional options for developing backups for your life and activities:

- ❏ Before you back up, clean out your old files. Delete older drafts and duplicates. There are software programs and apps that can help you.

- ❏ Back up your smartphone or at least certain aspects like the contact list you've built or the photos you take.

- ❏ Though this book is focused on personal emergency preparedness, if you work or have a business, plan for how you will continue to do business if your computer goes down.

Resources:

- Photo Organizers: www.appo.org

BACK UP YOUR HARD COPY FILES

- Vital Records

- Photographs and Memorabilia

- Important Documents

- Archived Documents

BACK UP YOUR COMPUTER DATA

The general backup strategy to follow:

3 copies — the original plus two backups

2 different media — the two backup copies should use different devices or formats. For example:

1 offsite copy — one copy should be stored offsite

28 Get Informed

Pick ONE action to take today:

- ❏ Learn how to access notifications on your cell phone.
- ❏ Get NOAA weather radio that uses batteries or has a battery backup.
- ❏ Confirm that your local sirens are working, if applicable.
- ❏ Get an app on your phone, such as the FEMA app or add the NWS mobile site to your home screen.

Possible Next Actions:

- ❏ Get involved with preparedness efforts at work, school, place of worship, or other organizations.

Resources:

- Fun ways to get informed:
  - www.cdc.gov/phpr/zombie/novel.htm
  - emergency.cdc.gov/socialmedia/zombies.asp
- Weather: mobile.weather.gov

Get Trained / Get Involved

Pick ONE action to take today:

- ❑ Take a CPR/AED course

- ❑ Take a First Aid course

- ❑ Find another resource for training and take your first course.

Possible Next Actions:

- ❑ Take more courses

- ❑ Volunteer with a disaster response or relief organization

Resources:

- Training and Volunteer Opportunities:
    - ○ American Red Cross: www.redcross.org/ux/take-a-class
    - ○ CERT: www.ready.gov/community-emergency-response-team
    - ○ VOAD: www.nvoad.org

- Training:
    - ○ CDC Education, Training, and Planning: Resources: www.cdc.gov/phpr/training.htm
    - ○ FEMA Independent Study: training.fema.gov/is

30 Prep for Recovery

Pick ONE action to take today:

- ❏ Read this Step and mark for reference

- ❏ Review any of the Appendices mentioned
    - o Appendix H — Safe Drinking Water
    - o Appendix J — Refrigerated Foods
    - o Appendix K — Frozen Foods
    - o Appendix L — Using Supplies Impacted by Flood Water
    - o Appendix M — Disaster-related Stress

- ❏ Purchase unscented liquid household bleach to clean undamaged canned goods after a flood. Check out Appendix L

- ❏ Add ONE more item to your emergency kit
    - o Work gloves
    - o Non-latex disposable gloves
    - o Non-latex gloves for dishwashing
    - o Sturdy shoes
    - o Long pants
    - o Ear plugs
    - o Sleep mask

- ❏ Call your insurance agent to talk about the recovery process in the event of a disaster. Some questions to ask are:
    - o when to call,
    - o what information they'll need,
    - o ask "what-if" a large-scale disaster happens and an agent isn't available to inspect in a timely manner, can you take pictures and begin clearing debris.

- ❏ Identify the disaster relief organization you will donate to or volunteer with (www.nvoad.org)

Possible Next Actions:

- ❏ Learn how to shut off your gas safely and get the right tools to do it.

- ❏ Begin training to volunteer with a disaster relief organization.

- ❏ Take a basic first-aid course to be better prepared to help others throughout the year.

HEALTH AND SAFETY

- ☐ Clean, safe water is a priority

- ☐ Food safety is important during and after a disaster.

- ☐ Use protective gear (aka PPE)

  - Gloves

    - o Puncture resistant gloves, such as leather work gloves or nitrile-coated gardening gloves, are necessary for handling debris.

    - o Stock non-latex disposable gloves for handling first aid needs and cleaning contaminated items.

    - o Add a pair or two of the heavy dishwashing gloves to your kit to use for cleaning. They are thicker, reusable if not punctured, and have longer cuffs to keep water out.

  - Shoes or boots

    - o Closed-toe, sturdy soled work boots or shoes that fit. You need these to protect you from puncture, dropped objects, and an uneven walking surface.

  - Long pants

    - o Protect your legs from cuts and punctures. I also suggest long sleeved shirts, but you may have to balance protection from cuts with preventing heat stress.

- ❏ Good wound care is important in preventing infections from contaminated debris, flood waters, and recoverable items.

  - Avoid contact. Always the easiest to say, but not necessarily the easiest to do. If you have open wounds, avoid contact with flood waters or standing water. Use protective gear (waterproof gloves and boots, etc.) and waterproof bandages.

- Apply immediate first aid to all wounds, even ones you consider minor, such as blisters, scrapes, or any break in the skin.

    o Wash your hands with soap and clean, running water, if possible. Hum the 'happy birthday song' twice.

    o Avoid touching the wound with your hands. Use disposable gloves if possible.

    o Stop the bleeding by applying direct pressure if necessary.

    o Clean the wound by gently flooding the wound with sterile saline solution, bottled water, or clean, running water.

    o Clean around the wound with soap and clean water.

    o Pat dry and apply bandage.

- Seek medical attention if:

    o The wound is an animal bite

    o The wound is a puncture by an object contaminated with soil, feces, saliva, or flood waters.

    o The wound is infected (painful, swollen, red, or draining)

Annual Check and Refresh

Pick ONE action to take today:

- ❑ Decide if you'll review and update once a year or spread it out, then — SCHEDULE it!

KEEP ITEMS UP-TO-DATE — WHICH STRATEGIES WILL YOU USE?

- ❑ Use the emergency stock as your backup supplies. You must make restocking a habit. Restock as you use items!

- ❑ Use your camping gear as part of your emergency supplies. Restock and add items you need after each camping trip.

- ❑ You can also check your kits more often. Check the contents twice a year when the clocks change.

- ❑ Schedule time once a year to check, review, and resupply all of your emergency preparedness supplies.

  Some notable events to tie your annual review to:

  - January — GO Month (Get Organized)
  - March — time change
  - May — start of hurricane season
  - June — Pet Preparedness Month
  - September — Preparedness Month
  - November — time change
  - Your birthday
  - End of the year
  - New Year

- ❑ Set up a monthly schedule to check certain sections of your emergency kits and supplies. Here's a suggested calendar.

  - January: Reinforce Habits (fill up the car, checking for building exits, change out the batteries, check fire extinguishers)

- February: Clothes and Personal (make sure the clothes still fit and are in good condition, wash them, replace or add personal items)

- March: Cooking and Evacuation Gear (get ready for grilling and camping season by checking your gear and your backup cooking plan)

- April: Financial (update PIC, rotate $, evaluate emergency funds)

- May: Home (shelter and supplies, review insurance, update home inventory, confirm high-wind preparations)

- June: Pets (emergency kit supplies, vaccinations, microchips, updated photos)

- July: Food and Water (refresh and update supplies)

- August: Grab & Go checklist (update)

- September: Emergency Kit (replace, refill, or add supplies)

- October: Computer and Phones (review backup plan and check emergency power supplies)

- November: Communications and Plans (update primary contacts and evacuation plans, remind family about communication plan and meet-up locations)

- December: Health (update your medicines, get your vaccinations and flu shot, refresh First Aid training)

❑ Create your own review schedule using some noteworthy days, weeks, and months.

SPECIFIC THINGS TO CHECK

❑ Check the product date of the food in your emergency kit and supplies. Replace products that may exceed their *Best-By* date if it's less than a year away. Refer to Appendix I — Best-By Dates to learn more.

❑ Replace the batteries in your emergency kits.

❑ Replace your smoke detector batteries at the same time. You can also follow the Change Your Clock / Change Your Batteries motto each spring and fall.

❑ Check on over-the-counter medications in your kits. Change out the old and add any new items you need. Check out Step #7 (Build a Kit — Medications), if you have questions about tossing expired medications.

❑ Update the clothes in your emergency kit. Your kids have grown. You may have lost or gained weight.

❑ Update your checklists, plans, contacts.

Acknowledge and Celebrate

Congratulations, you did it! You took 31 small steps toward organizing for emergencies and disasters. Take some time to thank someone who helped you with your journey (especially yourself).

You may not be done; however, you've made a great start.

Remember — the *everyday* disasters that can disrupt our lives. Are you ready for these?

- ❑ Car breakdown
- ❑ Tree falls on your house
- ❑ Water heater fails and floods your basement
- ❑ Stuck in traffic due to a major accident
- ❑ Power outage in your neighborhood that affects your business or work

Appendix A — Emergency Kit Supply List

<u>Emergency Kit</u>

❑ **Water*** (bottled or a water filter)

❑ **Medicine***

❑ **Cash**

❑ **Food** * **& Can Opener**

❑ **First Aid Kit & Guide**

❑ **Radio**

❑ **Flashlight**

❑ **Batteries**

❑ **Whistle**

❑ **Multi-purpose knife/tool**

❑ **Mask & Gloves** (at least 60% alcohol)

❑ **Hand Sanitizer**

❑ **Toilet Paper & Facial Tissues**

❑ **Personal Toiletries & Needs**

❑ **Change of Clothing**

❑ **PIC** (Personal Information Center notebook)

❑ **Extra Glasses**

❑ **Pencils, Pens, Games, Books, Paper, Toys**

* **enough for 3 days**
(or more)

<u>Records to put in your PIC</u>

❑ **Inventory list for insurance**

❑ **Recent photo of each person**

❑ **Medical contact information**

❑ **Copies of bills & accounts**

❑ **Copies of important papers**

❑ **And more – see Step #11**

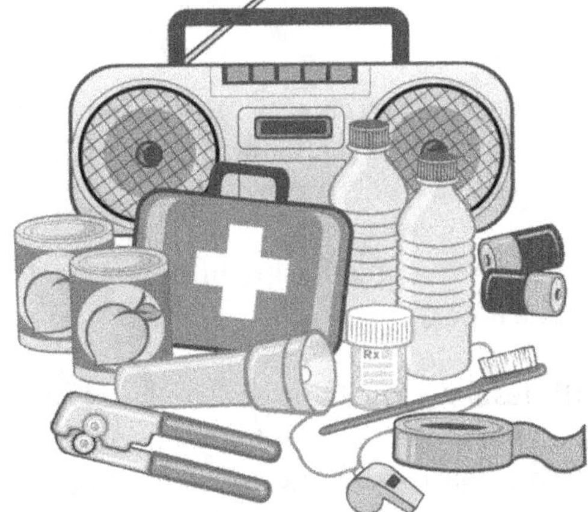

Your emergency kit should be portable so that if you have to evacuate, you have the basics that you need to survive for 3 days. We often leave our emergency kits at home, so think about and plan for an evacuation from your work if you are unable to return home.

To download a copy of this checklist, go to www.dhucks.com/emergencypreparedness.

More details on the emergency kit items.

ABSOLUTE NECESSITIES

- ❑ **Water** — A couple of bottles of water and an empty container. You will need one gallon per person per day for at least 3 days but since you won't be able to store that amount in this emergency kit, you should include an empty container you can fill or a personal water filter. Refer to Step #21 (Water)

- ❑ **Medicine** — Make sure you have your medicine with you. Ask your doctor and insurance company if you can get an extra refill to keep in your emergency kit. Make sure that you rotate it so it doesn't get old. Refer to Step # 7 (Build an Emergency Kit — Add Medications)

- ❑ **Cash** — Your ATM or credit card may not work, checks may not be accepted. Collect one-dollar bills over time until you have $200. We say cash is a necessity because you can buy almost everything else. Refer to Step #1 (Save Your Ones $)

REALLY GOOD IDEAS

- ❑ **Food and Can Opener** — You will need to stock more food in your home kit, but include something in your emergency kit. You could add snack bars that can withstand warm temperatures. There is nothing worse than gooey chocolate pooling at the bottom of the bag. Whether you add canned food to your emergency kit or not, add a can opener. You'll be ready when you get more supplies. Refer to Step #22 (Food).

- ❑ **First Aid Kit and Guide** — You can purchase one or make your own. Refer to Step #5 (First Aid Kit).

- ❑ **Radio** — Include a battery-operated or solar/wind-up powered radio with a NOAA Weather Radio All Hazards broadcast channel. Refer to Step #24 (Extras — Pick ONE).

- ❑ **Flashlight** — Stick with a battery-operated flashlight or lantern for your kit. The wind-up flashlights don't last as long.

- ❑ **Batteries** — Add extra batteries for your items and replace them annually. You could add the new ones to your emergency kit and use the old batteries in household items, such as remote controls, where you can replace them easily and your life doesn't depend on them. Seriously, no matter what the kids say — the remote control is not a life or death issue.

❑ **Whistle** — The whistle is intended to help you call for help without going hoarse. Refer to Step #24 (Extras — Pick ONE).

❑ **Multi-purpose tool** — Add a multi-purpose knife/tool because a knife, pliers, and a screw driver usually come in handy during an emergency. Choose one that is easy to hold and use rather than the one that has numerous tools but feels clumsy in your hand.

❑ **Mask & Gloves** — Add a nuisance dust mask, a surgical mask, and nitrile or vinyl gloves for first aid needs. Add leather or nitrile-covered gardening or work gloves for working with debris.

❑ **Hand Sanitizer** — (at least 60% alcohol). Hand hygiene is especially important in protecting your health. Since you may not be able to use soap and water, pack a container of hand sanitizer and maybe even some sanitizing towelettes.

❑ **Toilet Paper and Facial Tissues** — You can never go wrong with adding toilet paper to your emergency kit.

❑ **Personal Toiletries and Needs** — Pack an emergency version of a travel kit to include tooth brush and toothpaste (many things can be handled if you have a fresh mouth in the morning), deodorant, lotion, soap, shampoo, comb/brush, contact solutions, shaver, feminine hygiene products and anything else you can think of that can fit in the kit. Travel-sized items are perfect for this.

❑ **Important papers and documents in your PIC** — Keep your important papers safe, whether it's at home or in an offsite safe deposit box. Think flood as well as fire damage. Create a quick grab file notebook of the most important papers, mortgage, insurance, accounts, etc. to add to your emergency kit. This is your PIC (Personal Information Center), Step #11. Make copies of birth and marriage certificates. Create a list of contact information for doctors, bills and accounts.

NICE TO HAVE

❑ **Change of Clothing** — Add a change of clothing and clothes to sleep in if you have room. If you don't have much room, maybe some underwear and a pair of socks. There is a feeling of civilization if you have a clean pair of your own underwear available.

❑ **Extra pair of Glasses** — When you get a new pair of glasses, keep the old pair for your emergency kit.

❑ **Pencils, Pens, Games, Books, Paper, Toys** — This is intended to keep you entertained. If you have to evacuate, you won't have your normal routine to keep you occupied. If you have kids, they will definitely need something to play with, so add games, books, cards, and paper to write on. Make these physical games and books — power or batteries not required.

Appendix B — Emergency Kit for Pets

To download a copy of this checklist, go to www.dhucks.com/emergencypreparedness

Emergency Supply Kit for Pets

- ❑ **Water*** (bottled)
- ❑ **Food*** (canned or stored in an airtight, waterproof container)
- ❑ **Can opener** (if stocking canned food)
- ❑ **Medication**** (stored in an airtight, waterproof container)
- ❑ **First aid kit** (or add pet items to your main kit)
- ❑ **First aid book for pets** (my choice) ⟶
- ❑ **Travel bag, carrier, or crate** (one for each pet)
- ❑ **Anti-anxiety vest or wrap** (for each pet)
- ❑ **Collar/harness and leash with tags** (cats/dogs)
- ❑ **Long leash and yard stake** (dogs)
- ❑ **Litter tray and litter** (cats)
- ❑ **Poop bags** (dogs)
- ❑ **Food & water bowls**
- ❑ **Toys**

* enough for 3 – 7 days
** enough for 2 weeks

Records to add
- ❑ **Vet records**
- ❑ **Recent photo of pet**
- ❑ **Microchip records**
- ❑ **Vet contact information**

Appendix C — Grab & Go Checklist

GRAB

Priority Items

- ❑ Emergency Cash
- ❑ PIC Notebook *(Step #11)*
- ❑ Bill paying kit
- ❑ Passports and IDs
- ❑ Safety deposit key or home safe

Electronics

- ❑ Phones
- ❑ Phone chargers
- ❑ Batteries
- ❑ Flashlights and Lanterns
- ❑ Laptops
- ❑ Laptop power cords
- ❑ iPads/Tablets
- ❑ iPads/Tablets chargers
- ❑ Portable charger pack
- ❑ Camera & charger

Medication

- ❑ Prescription medication
- ❑ Any written prescriptions
- ❑ Equipment
- ❑ Pet medication
- ❑ Cold, Flu and Allergy medication
- ❑ Ibuprofen/Aspirin/Acetaminophen
- ❑ Supplements

Clothing

- ❑ Luggage
- ❑ Jeans, 1-2
- ❑ T-shirts, 1-2
- ❑ Long-sleeved shirt
- ❑ Pajamas
- ❑ Jacket or sweater
- ❑ Underwear
- ❑ Socks
- ❑ Walking shoes
- ❑ Flip flops
- ❑ Warm boots*
- ❑ Warm jacket*
- ❑ Hat and gloves*

PREP

Priority Items

- ❑ Gas up
- ❑ ATM — more cash
- ❑ Buy extra batteries

Electronics (if time)

- ❑ Charge phones
- ❑ Charge laptops
- ❑ Charge tablets
- ❑ Charge portable charger pack
- ❑ Forward home phone to cell phone, if applicable

Medication

- ❑ Charge any medical equipment with batteries

Clothing

* if winter

GRAB

Comfort and Hygiene

- ❑ Pillows**
- ❑ Blankets** (or sleeping bag)
- ❑ Toothbrush and toothpaste
- ❑ Personal hygiene products
- ❑ Toilet paper
- ❑ Trash bags

Dry Goods

- ❑ Coffee/Tea/Cocoa
- ❑ Sugar
- ❑ Canned meats
- ❑ Canned fruits
- ❑ Canned vegetables
- ❑ **Can opener**
- ❑ Peanut butter
- ❑ Crackers
- ❑ Individual snacks
- ❑ Water

Refrigerated and Frozen Foods

- ❑ Cooler(s)
- ❑ Blue Ice packs
- ❑ Frozen foods easily cooked
- ❑ Fruits and vegetables
- ❑ Deli meats
- ❑ cheeses
- ❑ Refrigerated foods that are safe if unrefrigerated for 4 hours or more

PREP

Comfort and Hygiene

** evacuation shelters may not have these

Dry Goods

- ❑ Fill water bottles

Refrigerated and Frozen Foods

- ❑ Buy ice
- ❑ Put a thermometer in cooler to ensure safe temperatures are maintained***

*** refer to Appendix J (Refrigerated Foods) and Appendix K (Frozen Foods) for safe temperatures

Appendix D — Digital Estate Planning

A digital estate plan is a plan for what happens to your digital assets which includes the social media accounts, email, banking apps, store rewards, and other accounts you listed in Step #12 (Your Digital Accounts — List Them) when you're gone. Your online accounts and assets are a part of your estate, but they may not be aware you have them.

Your family may need to access an account to turn off monthly payment for something you're not using anymore. You might prefer your email account to be deleted after your death.

Your spouse, children, parent or sibling may want to keep all those wonderful family photos you took and posted to your Facebook account or Flickr or stored in your Apple iCloud account. How will they access it? Will they lose these important mementos?

Have you ever had a "friend" suggestion on a social media account for someone you know has died? Do you want your profile to live on for years after you? You might, but you might also want it to be managed by your heirs.

Your online accounts are assets that need to be handled after you're gone. What do you want your heirs to do with it? A digital estate plan can be as detailed or as basic as you want it to be.

You started your digital estate plan in Step #12 (Your Digital Accounts — List Them) with the list of all your online/internet accounts. You may have made this list in paper or digital form and you are keeping it in a secure place. Adding your passwords and usernames for your accounts is the beginning of your digital estate plan.

The next step in building your digital estate plan is to check what each of your social media accounts say about what happens to your account on death or incapacity.

For example, does the sight allow you to assign a trusted individual to access and manage your account at your death. This contact would then be able to make decisions to delete your account or download a copy of photos and posts.

Check out what each of your social media accounts says about what happens to your account if you die or are incapacitated. Each social media and digital account is different so the best way to find out what you can do to develop your digital estate plan is to search using the word 'deceased' and the account you're working on.

More and more companies now have a policy in place on how family members can close or deactivate accounts. For example:

- Facebook allows you to have your account deleted when a family member requests it and provides proof of death and relationship. You can also choose a Legacy

Contact, who can then make additional decisions about the account once it is memorialized. That contact may be able to write one last message if you've allowed others to post to your timeline, update profile picture, and remove your account. I say *may* because by the time you read this, Facebook may have already changed their procedures.

- Google offers the opportunity to assign an Inactive Manager who will be notified that your accounts have been inactive for an amount of time you choose and will share any data you've chosen to share.

Your digital estate plan should include all online accounts you have (review the list in Step #12). If you include usernames and passwords — keep it secure. Let your executor know what you want done with each of your accounts, which accounts they are allowed to access using your username and password and which accounts require transfer of ownership. Include who to contact to make changes.

It's not just your retirement account that will require transfer of ownership. If you are a writer and have a published book on CreateSpace or KDP then your heir(s) are not allowed to access your account. But there is a process to transfer the account into a new account owned by them so they may continue to receive the royalties. Other assets may also require the transfer of the account to the heir(s) before the accounts can be accessed.

If there are other accounts that produce money, even if pennies a day, add them to the list and find out (and share the information) how the asset is transferred on death.

When your annual review of your will and digital estate plan is due, check up on what each of your account allows. Things change and a previous decision may no longer be the right one for you.

Possible Next Actions:

- ❏ Though this section was about digital estate planning, another action you can take is to draft or update your will. For help with a will, check out NOLO books, LegalShield, or contact your lawyer.

- ❏ Draft or update your medical power-of-attorney or living will. Most states provide a downloadable copy of the accepted format of living wills.

Appendix E — Family Communication Plan

Build your Family Communication Plan and include a copy in your PIC (Step #11), behind the first tab.

Family Communication Plan

Texts are more likely to get through.
Call 911 if it's an emergency

HOUSEHOLD INFORMATION

Home Phone: _______________

Name: ___________________________
Cell: ____________ Email: ____________
Social Media: _______________________
Other Information: ___________________
____

Name: ___________________________
Cell: ____________ Email: ____________
Social Media: _______________________
Other Information: ___________________
____

Name: ___________________________
Cell: ____________ Email: ____________
Social Media: _______________________
Other Information: ___________________
____

Name: ___________________________
Cell: ____________ Email: ____________
Social Media: _______________________
Other Information: ___________________
____

Pet: _______ / Pet: _______ / Pet: _______
Description: / Description: / Description:

Where Will You Meet?

In the Neighborhood: _______________
Address: _____________________________

In Town: _________________________
Address: _____________________________

Out of Town: _____________________
Address: _____________________________

Who's Your Contact?

Local: ____________________________
Home: ______________ / Cell: ___________
Email: ______________ / Social Media: _______
Out-of-Town: ______________________
Home: ______________ / Cell: ___________
Email: ______________ / Social Media: _______

WORK & SCHOOL

Work: _______________________________
Address: _____________________________
Phone: ______________________________
Social Media: _________________________
Emergency Plan/Pick-up: _______________

Work: _______________________________
Address: _____________________________
Phone: ______________________________
Social Media: _________________________
Emergency Plan/Pick-up: _______________

School: ______________________________
Address: _____________________________
Phone: ______________________________
Social Media: _________________________
Emergency Plan/Pick-up: _______________

School: ______________________________
Address: _____________________________
Phone: ______________________________
Social Media: _________________________
Emergency Plan/Pick-up: _______________

More Household Information

You can also use this for family
in another household

Name: _______________________________
Cell: _______________ Email: _______________
Social Media: _______________________________
Other Information: _______________________________
____

Name: _______________________________
Cell: _______________ Email: _______________
Social Media: _______________________________
Other Information: _______________________________
____

Name: _______________________________
Cell: _______________ Email: _______________
Social Media: _______________________________
Other Information: _______________________________
____

Name: _______________________________
Cell: _______________ Email: _______________
Social Media: _______________________________
Other Information: _______________________________
____

Pet: _______ | Pet: _______ | Pet: _______
Description: | Description: | Description:

Are You a Contact for Someone?

Name: _______________________________
Phone: _______________ / Social Media: _______________
Email: _______________________________

Other Important Numbers

Child Care: _______________________________
Address: _______________________________
Phone: _______________________________
Social Media: _______________________________
Emergency Plan/Pick-up: _______________________________

Senior Care: _______________________________
Address: _______________________________
Phone: _______________________________
Social Media: _______________________________
Emergency Plan/Pick-up: _______________________________

Friend: _______________________________
Neighbor: _______________________________

Doctor: _______________________________
Doctor: _______________________________
Doctor: _______________________________
Pharmacy: _______________________________
Dentist: _______________________________

Vet: _______________________________
Kennel: _______________________________

Poison Control: 1.800.222.1222

_______________ : _______________________________
_______________ : _______________________________
_______________ : _______________________________
_______________ : _______________________________

Create business cards with your emergency Meetup (Step #14) and your Check-In contacts (Step #15).

Where Will You Meet?

Neighborhood: _______________________________
Address: _______________________________

In Town: _______________________________
Address: _______________________________

Out of Town: _______________________________
Address: _______________________________

Who's Your Contact?

ICE / #: _______________________________

Local: _______________________________
Home: _______________ / Cell: _______________
Email: _______________ / Social Media: _______________

Out-of-Town: _______________________________
Home: _______________ / Cell: _______________
Email: _______________ / Social Media: _______________

Appendix F — Questions to Ask

Planning and preparing for emergencies and disasters requires you to think *what if...* and then take action to prevent possible outcomes from happening or add supplies and reminders (aka checklists) to be ready when something does happen. *What if...* also allows you to plan how you might respond during an emergency and what you might need to recover from a disaster.

Basic Questions to Identify Possible Hazards

- What disaster declarations have been made in my state in the last five years? Use www.fema.gov/disasters.

- Am I in a floodplain? In an area prone to earthquakes? Near a volcano?

- Is my community prone to seasonal hazards? Hurricanes, tornadoes, winter storms?

- There have been a few disasters in the news lately. Are they likely to occur in my area? If so, what would I do to prepare?

Expand to Include Other Times and Places

- *What if* there's a tornado warning at 2 pm on Tuesday? Where will I be?
  - Where would I go if I could see the twister?
  - Where are the other members of my family?
  - What will they do?
  - How will we communicate?

- *What if* I smell a gas leak at 9 pm on a Friday? What's the first thing I should do?
  - What does a gas leak smell like?
  - Who would I call? Is that number in my mobile phone?

- *What if* the smoke alarm goes off in the middle of the night? How will I get out of the house?
  - What's another way out of the room?
  - Where will we meet up?
  - If pets sleep in the room, what will I need to control them and get them safely out with me?

- *What if* I was stuck in traffic on the way to work or grocery shopping? What supplies might I need to have with me in the winter? In the summer?

Special Considerations

- What life-saving equipment, medicine, assistive devices, or treatment do I require?
    - Does it need power?
    - Does it need refrigeration?
    - Does it need space to maneuver?
    - If I can't go for my normal treatment, what happens? What's my backup?

- If I can't evacuate myself, who will I contact for assistance? What will I need to take with me?

- Are there any special dietary considerations I need to be prepared for if I'm not at home?

Make It a Game

- Whether you have kids or not, check out the games, puzzles, and resources at:
    - www.ready.gov/kids/games
    - www.nfpa.org/Public-Education
    - www.cdc.gov/phpr/readywrigley

- Make up your own board game, write questions on index cards, and roll the dice. Or have the kids create the game and play it together on Family Game Night.

Appendix G — Sheltering in Place for Other Hazards

Radiation, chemical, biological or pandemic hazards are less likely than the natural hazards we face each year. This book is intended to help you prepare for the more common hazards, but in case you want more information on the other hazards, here are some points to consider.

Choose a room for shelter

For radiation the best location is also an interior room or basement with the fewest windows and the most shielding (walls and ground) between you and the radiation source. The three factors that protect you from radiation is distance (more is better), shielding (more is better), and time (less time of exposure, but over time radiation levels drop). Interior rooms and basement spaces increases your shielding.

For chemical hazards, the best location is still an interior room but depending on the incident, a room higher in your house might be a better choice. If the chemical vapors are heavier than air, then they will lie low to the ground.

Other amenities to consider in choosing your shelter are adjoining bathroom facilities, wired phone line capability, and cell phone, television, and radio signal.

Turn on your radio and make sure you allow local emergency text updates on your mobile phone. Local officials will provide guidance and directions. Television may also be a good choice for information, directions and notice for 'all-clear'. But unless you are in the local area of the television station (i.e. live in the metropolitan area of the station) you may not get community specific information in a timely manner. Radio and a local station should be your first choice for information.

Gather supplies

For biological, chemical or radiological gather for sealing a room (if sheltering in place is advised):

- ❑ Plastic sheeting, 2-4 mil thickness.

  Pre-cut to the dimension of the window/door/vent plus at least 2 inches will save time. Mark each pre-cut sheet with a permanent marker for quick identification of placement.

- ❑ Duct tape

- ❑ Towels, bedding, etc. to use as additional barriers in front of doors.

For all situations:

- ❑ Sanitary supplies for pets (litter and box for cats, puppy pads or newspapers for dogs, plastic bags, etc.)

- ❑ Sanitary supplies for people if there's no bathroom available.

    - o 5-gallon bucket

    - o Heavy-duty plastic trash bags (use two)

    - o Cat litter

    - o Snap-on toilet seat and lid made for 5-gallon buckets

    - o Toilet paper or moist towelettes

    - o Moist towelettes and hand-sanitizer

    - o Twist ties

- ❑ Whistle.

    Having a whistle in your shelter, emergency kit, purse, backpack, car, and on your keychain. If you are trapped by debris, it is easier to indicate your position using your whistle than it is to yell. It saves energy and carries farther. Another option is an air horn.

Create a checklist of actions to take:

If you are sheltering in place to protect yourself from contaminated air your action checklist should include;

- ❑ High or Low? If you have the option of multiple shelters in your home, determine whether to shelter in the basement or a room in the top floor of your home based on the hazard. Some chemical hazards may be lighter than air and some may be heavier than air. When local officials provide directions and information, they'll tell you whether you should shelter in the lowest level or move to a higher level.

- ❑ Bring in outside animals if possible.

- ❑ Close and lock doors and windows. Locking provides a better seal against the contaminated air by pulling the door or window tighter.

- ❑ Turn off air handling equipment (air conditioners, fans, furnaces)

- ❑ Get emergency kit and emergency supplies, if not already present and it's not contaminated.

❑ If there is a possibility of radioactive contamination, prevent the contamination from entering your shelter by removing the outer layer of clothing (including shoes and accessories) before entering.

❑ Seal windows, doors, vents (air ducts, dryer vents, flues, etc.) with plastic sheeting and duct tape

❑ Listen to your radio for an all-clear announcement

❑ Unseal after several hours to prevent asphyxiation. You don't want to suffocate if the room is too tightly sealed for too long. Sealing your room is only a temporary action.

Other Actions to Take and Resources

Biological — www.ready.gov/Bioterrorism

❑ Install a High-Efficiency Particulate Air (HEPA) filter in your furnace return duct. The HEPA will filter out most biological agents that enter the house. Hire a professional to install the filter. If it is not sized and installed properly it will harm performance, shorten life of equipment and allow certain biological contaminants to go around the filter.

Pandemic — www.cdc.gov/nonpharmaceutical-interventions/pdf/gr-pan-flu-ind-house.pdf

❑ Stock your pantry with at least a two-week supply of food.

❑ Have any nonprescription drugs and other health supplies on hand. Don't wait to get sick to buy them. Include:

  o pain relievers,

  o stomach remedies,

  o cough and cold medicines,

  o fluids with electrolytes, and

  o vitamins.

❑ Have other items you use during an illness, including

  o hand soap,

  o facial tissues,

  o hand-sanitizer, at least 60% alcohol,

  o latex gloves, and

  o disposable facemask.

❏ Practice good personal health habits NOW

- o Stay home when you're sick.

- o Stay home at least another 24 hours after you no longer have a fever (without the use of meds).

- o Cover your coughs and sneezes with a tissue or your sleeve.

- o Wash your hands with soap and water for at least 20 seconds. Hum the 'happy birthday song' twice.

- o Clean frequently touched surfaces and objects

❏ Choose a room and a bathroom in your home that would be for the sole use of sick household members.

Appendix H — Safe Drinking Water

Treating water for microbial contamination

Here are several ways to disinfect water.

First, remove suspended particles: Before treating the water through one or more of the following techniques, allow the suspended particles to settle to the bottom and decant the clear liquid or strain the water through coffee filters, several layers of clean cloth, or paper towels.

Boiling:

1. Heat the water to a rolling boil (or roiling boil if you prefer), and continue boiling for a full minute. This will kill most microorganisms present in the water.

2. To improve the taste of the boiled water or bottled water that has been stored, mix in oxygen/air by pouring the water back and forth between two clean containers.

Boiling will not remove heavy metals or chemicals.

Chlorination: Plain household bleach — that is bleach with no added scent, cleaners or color safe ingredients — can be used to kill most microorganisms in the water. Use either the regular bleach that contains 5.25 to 6 percent sodium hypochlorite or the more common extra-strength bleach, which contains 8.25 percent sodium hypochlorite.

1. Add 6 drops or a little less than ⅛ teaspoon of 8.25% bleach per gallon of water. See table below for how many drops to use with other concentrations.

2. Stir and let stand 30 minutes. You want the water to have a slight bleach odor to it.

3. If it doesn't have a slight bleach odor, repeat and let stand for another 15 minutes.

4. If a slight odor is still not apparent, discard the water. There are more microorganisms and other contaminants in the water than the bleach can treat.

Note: sodium hypochlorite, the active ingredient in bleach, will break down into salt and water over time. The shelf-life of bleach is approximately one year if stored at room temperature. However, Clorox® recommends using bleach that is no older than four months to treat water. Other recommendations online are for six months. Shelf-life will be less at extreme cold or hot temperatures.

Buy the smallest bottle of bleach available. Then replace your bottle of bleach at least annually or when the use-by-date has passed, or if there is no smell of bleach when you measure it out (don't smell directly from the bottle). If you are unsure of the concentration of sodium hypochlorite, use 40 drops (or ½ teaspoon) of bleach.

How much bleach is needed to treat 1 gallon of water[3]:

% of sodium hypochlorite	Drops	Teaspoon (tsp)
5.25% - 6%	8 drops	a little less than ⅛ teaspoon
8.25%	6 drops	a little less than ⅛ teaspoon
unknown	40 drops	½ teaspoon

Chlorination will not remove heavy metals or chemicals.

Distillation: Distillation will remove heavy metals and most chemicals, along with any microbes present. Distillation involves boiling the water and then collecting the condensation. It requires a large canning or stock pot with a cover and a collection cup. You can rig a collection cup by turning the cover of the pot over so that the handle is inside the pot. Tie the cup to the handle so that it is hanging inside the pot, right-side up. The cup should not be in the water but above it. Boil the water for 20 minutes and collect the water that condenses in the cup. Unless you have a large stock pot or canning pot, a distillation set up is not going to be an option.

If your water comes from a private well or a cistern and has been contaminated, contact your local or state health department or agriculture extension agent for specific advice. You can also refer to CDC's guidance

- Cisterns and Other Rain Catchment Systems
  www.cdc.gov/healthywater/emergency/drinking/disinfection-cisterns.html

- Disinfection of Bored or Dug Wells After an Emergency
  www.cdc.gov/healthywater/emergency/drinking/disinfection-wells-bored.html

- Disinfection of Drilled or Driven Wells After an Emergency page at
  www.cdc.gov/healthywater/
  emergency/drinking/disinfection-wells-drilled.html

Resource

---

[3] Centers for Disease Control and Prevention (CDC), Making Water Safe in an Emergency, https://www.cdc.gov/healthywater/emergency/drinking/making-water-safe.html

- Emergency Water Supply
  www.cdc.gov/healthywater/emergency/drinking/creating-storing-emergency-water-supply.html

- Filters
    - www.cdc.gov/parasites/crypto/gen_info/filters.html
    - www.rei.com/learn/expert-advice/water-treatment-backcountry.html
    - www.rei.com/learn/expert-advice/water-treatment-international.html

- Making Water Safe in an Emergency
    - www.cdc.gov/healthywater/emergency/drinking/making-water-safe.html
    - www.ready.gov/water

Appendix I — Best-By Dates

Your milk has a *Sell By* date. Your crackers have a *Best When Used By* date, and your over-the-counter (OTC) pain reliever has an *Expiration* date. Does this mean the store has to pull these products off the shelf? Does it mean you shouldn't drink it, eat it, or take it? Not necessarily.

Here's some background on those best-by dates so that you can make the decision.

Whether it's food or medicine, storage temperature and humidity will effect the shelf life of the product. Higher temperatures and higher humidity will generally decrease the shelf life of the product. Freezing may also negatively effect some products. Follow the recommended storage instructions.

Food Product Dating

Dates are applied to food for **best quality** identification not for safety. These dates are not required by Federal regulations, except on infant formula. Infant formula is required to have a *Use-By* date and should not be used or bought after that date. Though product dating is not required (except for infant formula), all foods must be wholesome and fit for consumption regardless of product dating.

 If there is no sign of spoilage, all foods (except infant formula) may be purchased and consumed after the labeled product.

These dates are "open" product dates when the manufacturer has determined the product is at is **best quality**. For meat, poultry, eggs, and dairy these dates may contain only the month and the date. For shelf-stable and frozen products a year must also be displayed.

Dates on Egg Cartons

Sell By or *EXP* dates on eggs is not a federal regulation but may be required or prohibited by the state where the eggs are sold. There will also be a "pack date" on the carton if it has the USDA grade shield. Bring your smartphone with you to convert the code to a calendar date, as the pack date is a three-digit code identifying the consecutive day of the year (1 through 365). Example: February 19 is 050.

Dates on Cans

Though the "open" (*Sell By, Best When Used By*, etc.) is not required on cans and only indicates the date for the **best quality,** there must be a packing code which includes a "closed" date. This date is used for tracking the product and is the date the product was canned.

Discard cans that are deeply dented, rusted, or swollen. Tomatoes and fruits that are acidic will keep their **best quality** for 12 to 18 months. Less acidic products such as meats and vegetables will keep for two to five years. Store canned foods and other shelf stable products in a cool (below 85°F), dry place.

For more information, check out The USDA FSIS page, *Shelf-Stable Food Safety*, www.fsis.usda.gov/wps/portal/fsis/topics /food-safety-education/get-answers/food-safety-fact-sheets/safe-food-handling/shelf-stable-food-safety.

Expiration Dates for Medication

Expiration dates are listed on the medicine packages by the manufacturer. The date indicates how long the product is expected to remain stable and retain its strength, quality, and purity when it's been properly stored. Instructions for proper storage will usually indicate the accepted ranges of temperature and humidity.

Expiration dates may not necessarily mean you need to toss it. Here are a few rules of thumb:

- If your life depends on it — toss expired medication.

- If it has changed color, consistency or odor — toss it regardless of expiration.

- Don't take the aspirin if it smells like vinegar. It's one medication that should always be tossed when expired, or sooner if it smells like vinegar.

- Store medication in a cool, dry environment. Your bathroom medicine cabinet is rarely a good place.

For more information on expiration dates and medicine, check out this article from the Harvard Medical School Family Health Guide, www.health.harvard.edu/staying-healthy/drug-expiration-dates-do-they-mean-anything.

Resources

- Food Product Dating (*Best-By*): www.fsis.usda.gov/wps/portal/fsis/topics/food-safety-education/get-answers/food-safety-fact-sheets/food-labeling/food-product-dating/food-product-dating

- Food Safety: www.fsis.usda.gov/wps/portal/fsis/topics/food-safety-education/get-answers/food-safety-fact-sheets/safe-food-handling/shelf-stable-food-safety

- MREs: www.thereadystore.com/food-storage/7/what-is-the-shelf-life-of-mres/

- Medicines: www.health.harvard.edu/staying-healthy/drug-expiration-dates-do-they-mean-anything

Appendix J — Refrigerated Foods: When to Keep and When to Toss

FOOD	Held above 40°F for over 2 hours
MEAT, POULTRY, SEAFOOD	
Raw or leftover cooked meat, poultry, fish, or seafood; soy meat substitutes	Discard
Thawing meat or poultry	Discard
Meat, tuna, shrimp, chicken, or egg salad	Discard
Gravy, stuffing, broth	Discard
Lunchmeats, hot dogs, bacon, sausage, dried beef	Discard
Pizza, with any topping	Discard
Canned hams labeled "Keep Refrigerated"	Discard
Canned meats and fish, opened	Discard
CHEESE	
Soft Cheeses: blue/bleu, Roquefort, Brie, Camembert, cottage, cream, Monterey Jack, ricotta, mozzarella, etc.	Discard
Hard Cheeses: Cheddar, Colby, Swiss, Parmesan, provolone, Romano	Safe to Keep
Processed Cheeses	Safe to Keep
Shredded Cheeses	Discard
Low-fat Cheeses	Discard
Grated Parmesan, Romano, or combo (in can or jar)	Safe to Keep
DAIRY	
Milk, cream, sour cream, buttermilk, evaporated milk, yogurt, eggnog, soy milk	Discard
Butter, margarine	Safe to Keep
Baby formula, opened	Discard

FOOD	Held above 40°F for over 2 hours
EGGS	
Fresh eggs, hard-cooked in shell, egg dishes, egg products	Discard
Custards and puddings	Discard
CASSEROLES, SOUPS, STEWS	Discard
FRUITS	
Fresh fruits, cut	Discard
Fruit juices, opened	Safe to Keep
Canned fruits, opened	Safe to Keep
Fresh fruits, coconut, raisins, dried fruits, candied fruits, dates	Safe to Keep
SAUCES, SPREADS, JAMS	
Opened mayonnaise, tartar sauce, horseradish	Discard if above 50°F for over 8 hrs.
Peanut butter	Safe to Keep
Jelly, relish, taco sauce, mustard, catsup, olives, pickles	Safe to Keep
Worcestershire, soy, barbecue, Hoisin sauces	Safe to Keep
Fish sauces (oyster sauce)	Discard
Opened vinegar-based dressings	Safe to Keep
Opened creamy-based dressings	Discard
Spaghetti sauce, opened jar	Discard
BREAD, CAKES, COOKIES, PASTA, GRAINS	
Bread, rolls, cakes, muffins, quick breads, tortillas	Safe to Keep
Refrigerator biscuits, rolls, cookie dough	Discard
Cooked pasta, rice, potatoes	Discard
Pasta salads with mayonnaise or vinaigrette	Discard
Fresh pasta	Discard
Cheesecake	Discard
Breakfast foods-waffles, pancakes, bagels	Safe to Keep

FOOD	Held above 40°F for over 2 hours
PIES, PASTRY	
Pastries, cream filled	Discard
Pies-custard, cheese filled, or chiffon; quiche	Discard
Pies, fruit	Safe to Keep
VEGETABLES	
Fresh mushrooms, herbs, spices	Safe to Keep
Greens, pre-cut, pre-washed, packaged	Discard
Vegetables, raw	Safe to Keep
Vegetables, cooked; tofu	Discard
Vegetable juice, opened	Discard
Baked potatoes	Discard
Commercial garlic in oil	Discard
Potato salad	Discard

Source: United States Department of Agriculture (USDA), Keeping Food Safe During an Emergency, www.fsis.usda.gov/wps/portal/fsis/topics/food-safety-education/get-answers/food-safety-fact-sheets/emergency-preparedness/keeping-food-safe-during-an-emergency. Accessed 24 Nov. 2017.

Appendix K — Frozen Foods: When to Keep and When to Toss

FOOD	Still contains ice crystals and feels as cold as if refrigerated	Thawed. Held above 40°F for over 2 hours
MEAT, POULTRY, SEAFOOD		
Beef, veal, lamb, pork, and ground meats	Refreeze	Discard
Poultry and ground poultry	Refreeze	Discard
Variety meats (liver, kidney, heart, chitterlings)	Refreeze	Discard
Casseroles, stews, soups	Refreeze	Discard
Fish, shellfish, breaded seafood products	Refreeze Some texture and flavor loss	Discard
DAIRY		
Milk	Refreeze Some texture loss	Discard
Eggs (out of shell) and egg products	Refreeze	Discard
Ice cream, frozen yogurt	Discard	Discard
Cheese (soft and semi-soft)	Refreeze Some texture loss	Discard
Hard cheeses	Refreeze	Refreeze
Shredded cheeses	Refreeze	Discard
Casseroles containing milk, cream, eggs, soft cheeses	Refreeze	Discard
Cheesecake	Refreeze	Discard
FRUITS		
Juices	Refreeze	Refreeze Discard if mold, yeasty smell, or sliminess develops
Home or commercially packaged	Refreeze Some texture and flavor change	Refreeze Discard if mold, yeasty smell, or sliminess develops

FOOD	Still contains ice crystals and feels as cold as if refrigerated	Thawed. Held above 40°F for over 2 hours
VEGETABLES		
Juices	Refreeze	Discard if held above 40°F for 6 hours.
Home or commercially packaged or blanched	Refreeze Some texture and flavor loss	Discard if held above 40°F for 6 hours.
BREADS, PASTRIES		
Breads, rolls, muffins, cakes (without custard fillings)	Refreeze	Refreeze
Cakes, pies, pastries with custard or cheese filling	Refreeze	Discard
Pie crusts, commercial and homemade bread dough	Refreeze Some quality loss	Refreeze. Considerable quality loss
OTHER		
Casseroles-pasta, rice based	Refreeze	Discard
Flour, cornmeal, nuts	Refreeze	Refreeze
Breakfast items-waffles, pancakes, bagels	Refreeze	Refreeze
Frozen meal, entree, specialty items (pizza, sausage and biscuit, meat pie, convenience foods)	Refreeze	Discard

Source: United States Department of Agriculture (USDA), Keeping Food Safe During an Emergency, www.fsis.usda.gov/wps/portal/fsis/topics/food-safety-education/get-answers/food-safety-fact-sheets/emergency-preparedness/keeping-food-safe-during-an-emergency. Accessed 24 Nov. 2017.

Appendix L — Using Supplies Impacted by Flood Water

Flood waters may be contaminated with sewage and hazardous chemicals. Any items that come in contact with flood waters should be washed and decontaminated.

Cleaning Food Package (cans and retort packages)

You may not have to toss all your food even if it has come in contact with flood waters. Canned and "retort" packaged foods may be safe once the packaging has been cleaned and sanitized.

1. **Remove the labels** if possible. Dirt and bacteria may hide behind the label. Though the last step has you relabeling these items, you may need to mark them now in some way so you won't forget what is in each can or package.

2. **Remove any visible dirt** or mud.

3. **Wash** the cans and retort packages with soap and water. Use hot water if possible.

4. **Rinse** the packaged food with potable (safe to drink) water

5. **Sanitize** the cans and retort packages.

   - Place the packages and cans in a bleach solution. Use 1 cup of unscented, 5.25% household bleach for every 5 gallons of clean water. For the more concentrated bleach (8.25%) you can use ¾ cup per 5 gallons. Soak for at least 15 minutes.

6. **Air dry** sanitized cans and retort packages. Allow at least one hour before opening or storing.

7. **Relabel** with a permanent marking pen. Include the expiration date. If you don't re-label, you'll be enjoying a number of 'surprise' meals.

Resources

- Centers for Disease Control and Prevention (CDC), *Clean Up Safely After a Disaster:* www.cdc.gov/disasters/cleanup/facts.html

- Centers for Disease Control and Prevention (CDC), *Household Cleaning & Sanitizing:* www.cdc.gov/healthywater/emergency/cleaning-sanitizing/household-cleaning-sanitizing.html

- U.S. Food & Drug Administration (FDA), *How to Save Undamaged Food Packages Exposed to Flood Water:* www.fda.gov/food/resourcesforyou/consumers/ucm076881.htm#how

- U.S. Food & Drug Administration (FDA), *How to Save Undamaged Food Packages Exposed to Flood Water:* www.fda.gov/food/resourcesforyou/consumers/ucm076881.htm#how

Appendix M — Disaster–Related Stress

Recognize Signs of Disaster-Related Stress (www.ready.gov/coping-with-disaster)

When adults have the following signs, they might need crisis counseling or stress management assistance:

- Difficulty communicating thoughts.
- Difficulty sleeping.
- Difficulty maintaining balance in their lives.
- Low threshold of frustration.
- Increased use of drugs/alcohol.
- Limited attention span.
- Poor work performance.
- Headaches/stomach problems.
- Tunnel vision/muffled hearing.
- Colds or flu-like symptoms.
- Disorientation or confusion.
- Difficulty concentrating.
- Reluctance to leave home.
- Depression, sadness.
- Feelings of hopelessness.
- Mood-swings and easy bouts of crying.
- Overwhelming guilt and self-doubt.
- Fear of crowds, strangers, or being alone.

Helping Children Cope (www.ready.gov/kids/parents/coping)

- Listen to your kids. Validate their concerns.

- Answer questions simply and honestly.

- Be calm and reassuring.

- Allow children to contribute to the recovery plan. Everyone needs to feel they can contribute.

- Shut off the TV. Repeated images and stories about the disaster may cause additional stress. Children may think the emergency is not over.

- Stay connected and find support for your needs within your family, friends, community organizations, and faith-based groups. If you are supported, you're available to support your kids.

- Kids at different ages will react differently and will need different kinds of support and help to recover. Go to www.ready.gov/kids/parents/coping for more information on frequently asked questions for the different ages or developmental stages.

Helping Pets Recover

- Keep your pets under direct control until you've checked fences and cleared debris or other hazards.

- Allow service animals and pets plenty of uninterrupted sleep to recover.

- Re-establish routine activities as soon as possible.

- Provide favorite or familiar toys and enjoy some play time. It's good for both of you. Or spend some quiet time petting your animal.

Resources

- American Veterinary Medical Association (AVMA), www.avma.org/public/EmergencyCare/Pages/Pets-and-Disasters.aspx

- CDC, emergency.cdc.gov/coping/index.asp

- Ready.gov: www.ready.gov/coping-with-disaster

- Ready.gov: www.ready.gov/kids/parents/coping

- Substance Abuse and Mental Health Services Administration (SAMHSA): www.samhsa.gov/disaster-preparedness

Appendix N — Car Emergency Kit

To download a copy of this checklist, go to www.dhucks.com/emergencypreparedness

Emergency Supplies for Your Car

In addition to an Emergency Kit add:

- ❑ **Jumper Cables** or better yet – a Portable Jump Starter
- ❑ **Flares or reflective triangle**
- ❑ **Car cell phone charger**
- ❑ **Flashlight**
- ❑ **Leashes** (if you travel with pets)

In WINTER add:

- ❑ **Ice scraper**
- ❑ **Warm coat**
- ❑ **Warm boots**
- ❑ **Extra gloves, hat, and scarf**
- ❑ **Blanket**
- ❑ **Cat litter or sand** for traction
- ❑ **Snow shovel**

Also
- ❑ **Fill up your gas tank at half-empty**
- ❑ **Keep tires inflated**
- ❑ **Check-up & fill fluids before trips**

Appendix O — Business Continuity Planning — Basics

You may own a business, be an employee at a company, or be self-employed. This book is not intended to cover emergency planning for businesses, however, if your business or employer is impacted by an emergency or disaster, your life and livelihood will also be affected. Here are five general areas to review and questions to ask to help your business prepare for emergencies and disasters. Go to www.ready.gov/business for more information.

INSURANCE

What coverage do you HAVE? What coverage do you NEED?

Insurance Coverage	HAVE?	NEED?
Electronic Data Recovery	☐	☐
Business Property	☐	☐
Flood or Water Damage	☐	☐
Power Outage Losses	☐	☐
Business Interruption	☐	☐
Service Interruption (utilities)	☐	☐

❑ Make an up-to-date inventory (video, photos, list)

Resources: your insurance agent and other agents in your network

DATA

Is it backed up? Use the 3-2-1 Backup Strategy

- ❑ 3 copies

- ❑ 2 different media

- ❑ 1 offsite copy

What's your PLAN B if …?

- Your laptop/computer crashes

- There's no power

How secure is your data?

Resources: www.staysafeonline.org and your computer expert

MONEY (Income & Expenses)

What do you need to stay in business?

- Income / Customers

- Supplies / Vendors

- Products & Services / Employees

What's the PLAN B if you can't work in your "office"?

What's your vendor's PLAN B if they can't deliver?

What's your PLAN B for paying employees, vendors, and receiving payment if there's no power?

What if your website goes down?

Resources: your Profit & Loss Statement, your accountant & web designer

COMMUNICATION

How will you communicate with...?

- Employees

- Customers

- Vendors

- Community / Organizations

PEOPLE

What's your communication plan? See COMMUNICATION (above).

What's your plan for working off-site? See MONEY (above).

Are your employees, vendors, and customers prepared? How can you help them be better prepared?

For detailed business continuity planning go to www.ready.gov/business.

Appendix P — Hazards & Mitigation

Resources to plan for and mitigate the following hazards

- ❏ Active Shooter — if you have children in school, does the school have an Active Shooter plan?

    - o www.ready.gov/active-shooter

        1. RUN and escape, if possible.

        2. HIDE, if escape is not possible

        3. FIGHT as an absolute last resort

- ❏ Bioterrorism

    - o www.ready.gov/Bioterrorism

- ❏ Chemical Emergencies (terrorist attack with chemical agents)

    - o www.ready.gov/chemical

- ❏ Cyber Security

    - o www.ready.gov/Cyber-Security

- ❏ Dam/Levee Failure

    - o See Floods, www.ready.gov/floods

- ❏ Drought

    - o www.ready.gov/drought

- ❏ Earthquakes

    - o www.ready.gov/earthquakes

        1. DROP

        2. COVER

        3. HOLD ON

- ❏ Explosions

    - o www.ready.gov/explosions

- ❏ Extreme Heat (heat wave)
    - o www.ready.gov/heat
- ❏ Floods
    - o www.ready.gov/floods
- ❏ Gremlins
    - o Don't get them wet or feed them after midnight
- ❏ Hazardous Materials Incidents — do you live near railway or a road with truck traffic?
    - o www.ready.gov/hazardous-materials-incidents
- ❏ House Fires
    - o www.ready.gov/home-fires
- ❏ Household Chemical Emergencies
    - o www.ready.gov/household-chemical-emergencies
- ❏ Hurricanes
    - o www.ready.gov/hurricanes
    - o www.fema.gov/pdf/media/factsheets/2011/avoiding_hurricane_damage.pdf
    - o www.fema.gov/residential-safe-rooms
    - o www.fema.gov/fema-p-320-taking-shelter-storm-building-safe-room-your-home-or-small-business
    - o www.nhc.noaa.gov/climo/
    - o www.nhc.noaa.gov/aboutsshws.php
- ❏ Landslides and Debris Flow
    - o www.ready.gov/landslides-debris-flow
- ❏ Nuclear Blast
    - o www.ready.gov/nuclear-blast

- ❑ Nuclear Power Plants

  - o www.ready.gov/nuclear-power-plants

- ❑ Pandemic

  - o www.cdc.gov/nonpharmaceutical-interventions/pdf/gr-pan-flu-ind-house.pdf

  - o www.ready.gov/pandemic

- ❑ Power Outages

  - o www.ready.gov/power-outages

- ❑ Radiation and Radiological Dispersion Device

  - o www.ready.gov/radiological-dispersion-device

  - o emergency.cdc.gov/radiation/index.asp
    1. GET INSIDE
    2. STAY INSIDE
    3. STAY TUNED

- ❑ Severe Weather

  - o www.ready.gov/severe-weather

- ❑ Snowstorms and Extreme Cold

  - o www.ready.gov/winter-weather

- ❑ Space Weather — solar flares and coronal mass ejections can effect the performance of technology on Earth.

  - o www.ready.gov/space-weather

- ❑ Terrorism

- ❑ Thunderstorms and Lightning

  - o www.ready.gov/thunderstorms-lightning

- ❑ Tornadoes
    - o www.ready.gov/tornadoes
    - o www.fema.gov/residential-safe-rooms
    - o www.fema.gov/fema-p-320-taking-shelter-storm-building-safe-room-your-home-or-small-business
- ❑ Tribbles
    - o DO NOT feed them
- ❑ Tsunamis
    - o www.ready.gov/tsunamis
- ❑ Volcanoes and lava flow (volcanic eruption)
    - o www.ready.gov/volcanoes
- ❑ Wildfires
    - o www.ready.gov/wildfires
- ❑ Zombies
    - o www.cdc.gov/phpr/zombie/novel.htm
    - o emergency.cdc.gov/socialmedia/zombies.asp

Glossary

Term	Definition
AED	Automated External Defibrillator
CDC	Centers for Disease Control and Prevention
CERT	Community Emergency Response Team
Chunk of Time	A small period of time in which you work. This time period is small enough to keep you willing to organize, but large enough to make progress. It's intended to break up a larger block of time and help you refocus on your original goal or intention. 15 minutes is a natural chunk of time, but 20, 23, and 30 minutes are also common. However, 5, 7, and 10 minutes can also be used if that's all the time you have.
CPO-CD®	Certified Professional Organizer in Chronic Disorganization. Certified from the Institute for Challenging Disorganization. The CPO-CD® certified individual is a professional organizer who has been educated in depth on the issues of chronic disorganization.
CPR	Cardiopulmonary Resuscitation
Disaster	A situation that overwhelms available resources.
Disinfect	Destruction or removal of illness causing germs (bacteria and viruses). Methods include heat, chemicals, ultraviolet (UV) light, and solar radiation. Filtration may remove bacteria but not viruses from the water if the filter size is between 0.1 and 0.4 microns. Reverse osmosis and newer filtration technology may remove viruses.
Emergency	A situation that calls for immediate action or assistance.
FEMA	Federal Emergency Management Agency, part of the U.S. Department of Homeland Security (DHS)

Term	**Definition**
Filter (water)	Physically remove illness causing germs (protozoa, cysts, bacteria, and viruses) and particles. The size of the filter pores determines which germs and particles are removed. See *germs* for more details.
Flood Watch	**Be Aware.** Conditions are right for flooding to occur in your area.
Flood Warning	**Take Action!** Flooding is either happening or will happen shortly.
Grab & Go Checklist	A checklist of priority items to take with you when you evacuate that cannot be left in your emergency kit.
Hazard Mitigation	Removing or reducing a potential vulnerability in your home and workplace.
HEPA Filter	High-Efficiency Particulate Air filter
Hurricanes	A hurricane is a tropical cyclone, which is a rotating, organized system of clouds and thunderstorms that originates over tropical or subtropical waters and has a closed low-level circulation. Tropical cyclones rotate counterclockwise in the Northern Hemisphere. They are classified as follows: **Tropical Depression:** A tropical cyclone with maximum sustained winds of 38 mph (33 knots) or less. **Tropical Storm:** A tropical cyclone with maximum sustained winds of 39 to 73 mph (34 to 63 knots). **Hurricane:** A tropical cyclone with maximum sustained winds of 74 mph (64 knots) or higher. In the western North Pacific, hurricanes are called typhoons; similar storms in the Indian Ocean and South Pacific Ocean are called cyclones.

Term	Definition
Term	**Definition**

Term	Definition
Hurricanes continued	**Major Hurricane:** A tropical cyclone with maximum sustained winds of 111 mph (96 knots) or higher, corresponding to a Category 3, 4 or 5 on the Saffir-Simpson Hurricane Wind Scale.

Category 1   74-95 mph

Category 2   96-110 mph

Category 3   111-129 mph

Category 4   130-156 mph

Category 5   157+ mph

Saffir-Simpson Hurricane Wind Scale is a 1 to 5 rating based on a hurricane's sustained wind speed.

Term	Definition
IATA	International Air Transportation Association
Mass Care Shelter	Shelter and services provided to a large number of people displaced by an emergency or disaster. It may be a temporary place to shelter during the hazard, such as a tornado. It may be open for a longer time period and provide food, bedding, and other care.
OTC	Over-the-counter medicines such as aspirin, cough medicine, etc.
Personal Information Center (PIC)	A physical notebook or a digital file containing essential personal information and important records such as copies of utility bills, bank and credit card statements, medical history, wills, birth certificates, death certificates and other vital documents.
PIC	Personal Information Center

Term	**Definition**
Retort package	Food packaging made from laminates of flexible plastics and metals. Common in MREs (Meals, Ready-to-Eat), camping food, and individual servings of juices.

Image By Bahamut0013 (Own work) [CC BY 3.0 (http://creativecommons.org/licenses/by/3.0)], via Wikimedia Commons

Term	**Definition**
Rx	Prescription, medicine prescribed by a physician.
Safe Room	A hardened structure specifically designed to meet Federal Emergency Management Agency (FEMA) criteria and provide near-absolute protection in extreme weather events, including tornadoes and hurricanes.
Shelter	Protection from the weather or other hazards. The best shelter option depends on the hazard. You may need to shelter for a few hours or for days and weeks. You may need to stay put and shelter in place, whether it's at home, work, school, out in your community, or traveling. You may need to evacuate and seek shelter with family, friends, or a hotel outside of the affected area. You may need to go to a community or mass care shelter with other residents affected by emergency or disaster.
Shelter in Place	Staying put and sheltering from the hazards where you are. You may need to shelter in place at home, work, school, or out in the community. You may be traveling or visiting and need to shelter in place.
Someday	A period of time that never arrives.

Term	**Definition**

Timer — An essential tool for refocusing on what you intended to do, rather than what drew your attention away. Basic requirements are an auditory or vibrational indication at the end of your chunk of time to remind you, "Hey! Get back to what you said you wanted to do right now! "

Trimline corded phone —

Photo by Donald Genaro (Own work) [CC BY-SA 3.0 (https://creativecommons. org/licenses/by-sa/3.0)], via Wikimedia Commons

also known as slimline or princess phone.

VOAD — Voluntary Organizations Active in Disaster (www.nvoad.org)

VoIP phone — Voice over Internet Protocol phone

Warning (weather) — **Reminder that a Watch is "lower" than a Warning**

A **warning** means that a weather emergency is already happening, or will happen soon. When you hear a warning, take immediate action.

Extreme Wind Warning: Extreme sustained winds of a major hurricane (115 mph or greater), usually associated with the eyewall, are expected to begin within an hour. Take immediate shelter in the interior portion of a well-built structure.

Flash Flood Warning: Issued when a flash flood has been reported or is imminent.

Flood Warning: Issued as an advance notice that a flood is imminent or is in progress at a certain location or in a certain river basin.

Term	Definition

Term   **Definition**

Warning (weather) continued

Severe Thunderstorm Warning: Indicates that severe thunderstorms have been sighted in your area.

Storm Surge Warning: There is a danger of life-threatening inundation from rising water moving inland from the shoreline somewhere within the specified area, generally within 36 hours. If you are under a storm surge warning, check for evacuation orders from your local officials.

Tornado Warning: A tornado has been sighted or radar indicates. Shelter immediately.

Tropical Storm Warning: Tropical storm conditions (sustained winds of 39 to 73 mph) are expected within your area within 36 hours.

Sources:

- www.cdc.gov/phpr/areyouprepared/informed.htm
- www.nws.noaa.gov/om/hurricane/ww.html
- www.ready.gov/tornadoes

Watch (weather)

Remember a Warning is more "serious/imminent" than a Watch

A **watch** means that there is a high possibility that a weather emergency will occur. When a severe storm watch is issued for your area, continue to listen to the radio or television for updates and pay attention to visible weather changes around you.

Flash Flood Watch: Issued when flash flooding is possible within the designated watch area.

Hurricane Watch: Hurricane conditions (sustained winds of 74 mph or greater) are possible within your area. Because it may not be safe to prepare for a hurricane once winds reach tropical storm force, The NHC issues hurricane watches 48 hours before it anticipates tropical storm-force winds.

Term	Definition

Watch (weather)

Severe Thunderstorm Watch: Indicates that conditions are right for:

- o Lightning or damaging winds greater than 58 mph,
- o Hail that could reach a diameter of 0.75 inches, and
- o Heavy rain.

Storm Surge Watch: There is a possibility of life-threatening inundation from rising water moving inland from the shoreline somewhere within the specified area, generally within 48 hours. If you are under a storm surge watch, check for evacuation orders from your local officials.

Tornado Watch: Tornadoes are possible. Move near enough to a shelter or sturdy building that you can reach it quickly if you see a tornado or the Watch becomes a Warning. Watch the sky and stay tuned to weather alerts.

Tropical Storm Watch: Tropical storm conditions (sustained winds of 39 to 73 mph) are possible within the specified area within 48 hours.

Evacuate if told to do so.

Sources:

- www.cdc.gov/phpr/areyouprepared/informed.htm

- www.nws.noaa.gov/om/hurricane/ww.html

- www.ready.gov/tornadoes

Wireline phone

Standard landline phone that is wired and not VoIP (Voice Over Internet Protocol) or wireless cellular phone service.

Resources

- 1Password, 1password.com [password manager]

- 911PetChip™, 911petchip.com [microchip manufacturer]

- 911PetChip™, www.FreePetChipRegistry.com [registration]

- American Animal Hospital Association (AAHA), www.petmicrochiplookup.org [Universal Pet Microchip Lookup Tool]

- American Red Cross, www.redcross.org/about-us/our-work/training-education [First Aid and CPR training]

- American Red Cross: www.redcross.org/ux/take-a-class [training and volunteer opportunities]

- American Society for the Prevention of Cruelty to Animals (ASPCA), www.aspca.org/pet-care/general-pet-care/disaster-preparedness [preparedness for birds, reptiles, horses, and small animals]

- American Veterinary Medical Association (AVMA): www.avma.org/public/EmergencyCare/Pages/Pets-and-Disasters.aspx [pets and disasters]

- Association of Personal Photo Organizers (APPO): www.appo.org [help with photos]

- Avid™, avidid.com [microchip manufacturer]

- Avid™, avidid.com/pettrac/enrollment [registration]

Centers for Disease Control and Prevention (CDC)

- www.cdc.gov/disasters/cleanup/facts.html [*Clean Up Safely After a Disaster*]

- emergency.cdc.gov/coping/index.asp [coping]

- www.cdc.gov/parasites/crypto/gen_info/filters.html [filters]

- www.cdc.gov/phpr/zombie/novel.htm [fun ways to get informed]

- emergency.cdc.gov/socialmedia/zombies.asp [fun ways to get informed]

- emergency.cdc.gov [general emergency preparedness]

- www.cdc.gov/nonpharmaceutical-interventions/pdf/gr-pan-flu-ind-house.pdf [*Get Your Household Ready for Pandemic Flu*]

- www.cdc.gov/healthywater/emergency/cleaning-sanitizing/household-cleaning-sanitizing.html [*Household Cleaning & Sanitizing*]

- www.cdc.gov/vaccines/schedules/easy-to-read/adult.html [immunizations]

- www.cdc.gov/tetanus/index.html [tetanus]

Centers for Disease Control and Prevention (CDC) cont.

- www.cdc.gov/phpr/training.htm [training]

- www.cdc.gov/healthywater/emergency/drinking/creating-storing-emergency-water-supply.html [water]

- www.cdc.gov/healthywater/emergency/drinking/making-water-safe.html [water]

- www.cdc.gov/healthywater/emergency/drinking/disinfection-cisterns.html [water — cisterns or rain catchment]

- www.cdc.gov/healthywater/emergency/drinking/disinfection-wells-bored.html [water — bored or dug wells]

- www.cdc.gov/healthywater/emergency/drinking/disinfection-wells-drilled.html [water — drilled or driven wells]

- Department of Homeland Security (DHS), www.dhs.gov/wireless-priority-service-wps [who gets priority access]

Department of Homeland Security (Ready campaign)

- www.ready.gov/alerts [alerts]

- www.ready.gov/bioterrorism [bioterrorism]

- www.ready.gov/business [business continuity planning]

- www.ready.gov/coping-with-disaster [*Coping with Disaster*]

- ready.gov [general emergency preparedness]

- www.ready.gov/kids/parents/coping [*Helping Children Cope*]

- www.ready.gov/individuals-access-functional-needs [*Individuals with Disabilities*]

- www.ready.gov/tornadoes [tornadoes]

- www.ready.gov/community-emergency-response-team [training and volunteer opportunities — CERT]

- www.ready.gov/water [water]

- Drug Enforcement Administration (DEA), takebackday.dea.gov [local drug take back locations]

- Dhucks, www.dhucks.com/emergencypreparedness [download various resources]

- Environmental Protection Agency (EPA), www.epa.gov/sites/production/files/2015-06/documents/how-to-dispose-medicines.pdf [disposal]

- Facebook, www.facebook.com/about/safetycheck [safety check]

Federal Emergency Management Agency (FEMA)

- www.fema.gov/integrated-public-alert-warning-system [alerts]

- www.fema.gov/media-library/assets/documents/26975 [alerts]

- www.fema.gov/media-library-data/1390856235302-ff6e316df62851d5a5afe834b4fcd53c/Commuter_Emergency_Plan_v7_508.pdf [commuter emergency plan]

- www.disasterassistance.gov [disaster assistance]

- www.fema.gov/disasters [disaster search by State/Territory]

- www.fema.gov/media-library-data/1420417719892-b9b41636569f3c41eea88e70ddfae2e2/FEMA528.pdf [*Earthquake Home Hazard Hunt*]

- www.fema.gov/media-library/assets/documents/6015 [earthquakes]

- www.fema.gov/media-library/assets/documents/109669 [flooding]

- www.fema.gov/pdf/media/factsheets/2011/avoiding_hurricane_damage.pdf [hurricanes and hurricane clips]

- www.fema.gov/disaster/updates/hurricane-maria-rumor-control [rumor control]

- www.fema.gov/safe-rooms [safe room]

- www.fema.gov/residential-safe-rooms [safe room]

- www.fema.gov/fema-p-320-taking-shelter-storm-building-safe-room-your-home-or-small-business [safe room]

- training.fema.gov/is [training]

- Harvard Health Publishing, Harvard Medical School, www.health.harvard.edu/staying-healthy/drug-expiration-dates-do-they-mean-anything [expiration dates]

- Institute for Challenging Disorganization, challengingdisorganization.org [professional organizers trained to help clients with chronic disorganization]

- International Air Transport Association (IATA), www.iata.org/whatwedo/cargo/live-animals/pets /Pages/index.aspx [guidance for dimensions of container]

- LastPass, www.lastpass.com [password manager]

- Microchip ID Solutions Inc., microchipidsolutions.com [microchip manufacturer and registration]

- National Association of Productivity and Organizing Professionals (NAPO), www.napo.net [help with preparedness]

- NAPO Virtual Chapter, www.virtualorganizers.com [professional organizers who work with you off-site or virtually]

- National Oceanic and Atmospheric Administration (NOAA), National Weather Service, www.nws.noaa.gov/nwr [alerts]

- National Weather Service (NWS), mobile.weather.gov [weather forecasts and updates]

- OutdoorGearlLab, www.outdoorgearlab.com/topics /camping-and-hiking/best-cooler/buying-advice [coolers]

- Poison Control Center, www.PoisonHelp.org

- The Ready Store, www.thereadystore.com/food-storage/7/what-is-the-shelf-life-of-mres [MREs]

- Recreational Equipment, Inc. (REI), www.rei.com/learn /expert-advice/water-treatment-backcountry.html [filters]

- Recreational Equipment, Inc. (REI), www.rei.com/learn /expert-advice/water-treatment-international.html

- Shake Out™, www.shakeout.org [earthquake]

- Stay Safe Online, National Cyber Security Alliance (NCSA), staysafeonline.org/stay-safe-online/securing-key-accounts-devices/passwords-securing-accounts [how to stay secure and safe online]

- Substance Abuse and Mental Health Services Administration (SAMHSA), www.samhsa.gov/disaster-preparedness [behavioral health resources]

U.S. Department of Agriculture (USDA), Food Safety and Inspection Service

- www.fsis.usda.gov/wps/portal/fsis/topics/food-safety-education/get-answers/food-safety-fact-sheets/food-labeling/food-product-dating/food-product-dating [product dating (*Best-By*)]

- www.fsis.usda.gov/wps/portal/fsis/topics/food-safety-education/get-answers/food-safety-fact-sheets/safe-food-handling/shelf-stable-food-safety [food safety]

- www.fsis.usda.gov/wps/portal/fsis/topics/food-safety-education/get-answers/food-safety-fact-sheet/emergency-preparedness/keeping-food-safe-during-an-emergency [food safety during an emergency]

U.S. Food & Drug Administration (FDA)

- www.fda.gov/ForConsumers/ConsumerUpdates/ucm101653.htm [disposal of unused medicines]

- www.fda.gov/food/resourcesforyou/consumers/ucm076881.htm#how [*How to Save Undamaged Food Packages Exposed to Flood Water*]

Volunteer Organizations Active in Disasters (VOAD)

- www.nvoad.org [disaster assistance and volunteer opportunities]
- www.nvoad.org/howtohelp [helping others]
- YouTube, youtu.be/h8CwNyfaU3g [emergency muzzle]

Resources located on the Dhucks.com website

- Resources and links mentioned in this guide, www.dhucks.com/resource-links-preparedness
- Blog, www.dhucks.com/blog

Additional Dhucks' resources

- Facebook: www.facebook.com/DHUCKSinaRow
- Pinterest: www.pinterest.com/shawndraholmber

Images

Page	Photo	Attribution
110	Retort bag	Image By Bahamuto013 (Own work) [CC BY 3.0 (http://creativecommons.org/licenses/by/3.0)], via Wikimedia Commons
111	Trimline corded phone	Photo by Donald Genaro (Own work) [CC BY-SA 3.0 (https://creativecommons.org/licenses/by-sa/3.0)], via Wikimedia Commons

Keyword Index

so, who's this shawndra person, anyway?

Shawndra Holmberg has been organizing longer than the eleven years she's been running her business, **Dhucks**. She believes in the power that an organized space, schedule, and life have on our creative spirit. She knows there's not one right way to get organized, and she's trained to make your organization work for you. She is a Certified Professional Organizer in Chronic Disorganization (CPO-CD®) and is focused on being your personal trainer for productivity, a mentor for your goals, and a motivational force for your creativity.

On her journey to becoming an organizer, Shawndra tackled jobs as varied as bioterrorism preparedness planner for the Hawai'i State Department of Health on the Big Island, coordinated environmental and safety training on Johnston Atoll (approximately 850 miles southwest of Hawai'i), and handled health and safety issues for a year at the South Pole station, Antarctica, with temperatures ranging from a balmy -7°F to a chilling -112°F.

Shawndra considers herself a lousy tourist as she usually spends her vacations enjoying a good book (reading one or writing one) and drinking coffee on her lanai, deck, porch, or sunroom. That's why she prefers to live and work in interesting locales. She spent a year at the South Pole, Antarctica, attended graduate school in big sky country (Bozeman, Montana), worked on Johnston Island, and then thawed out in Hawai'i. She is currently enjoying the people and scenery of Western Pennsylvania as she organizes and coaches writers and others who are reaching for their dream. She is located in Pennsylvania but works virtually everywhere.

If you would like an email when Shawndra's next book is released, sign up www.dhucks.com/newreleases. Your email address will never be shared and you can unsubscribe at any time.

If you enjoyed this book, please consider leaving a review on Amazon or Goodreads. A line or two or just the stars rating would make all the difference in helping others find this resource so they can prepare for emergencies and disasters too.

and what's this about a dhuck?

Dhucks are fun, playful and cute. What better mascot for organizing or *getting your dhucks in a row*. Shawndra has had a life-long interest in getting her dhucks in a row, whether it's getting organized, losing weight, reaching for a dream, or finding the joy in each day. Join the fun and *get your dhucks in a row*.

books by
Shawndra Holmberg

31 Small Steps to Organize Your Life
31 Small Steps to Organize for Weight Loss
31 Small Steps to Organize Your Paper
31 Small Steps to Organize for Emergencies (and Disasters)